BK
THE SAGA BEGINS

LEO MOORE

Bk
The Saga Begins

Copyright © 2020 by Leo Moore.

Paperback ISBN: 978-1-952982-92-7
Ebook ISBN: 978-1-952982-51-4

All rights reserved. No part in this book may be produced and transmitted in any form or by any means, electronic, or mechanical, including photocopying, recording, or by any information storage and retrieval system, without permission in writing from the copyright owner.

The views expressed in this work are solely those of the author and do not necessarily reflect the views of the publisher hereby disclaims any responsibility for them.

Published by Golden Ink Media Services   10/31/2020

Golden Ink Media Services
(302) 703-7235
support@goldeninkmediaservices@gmail.com

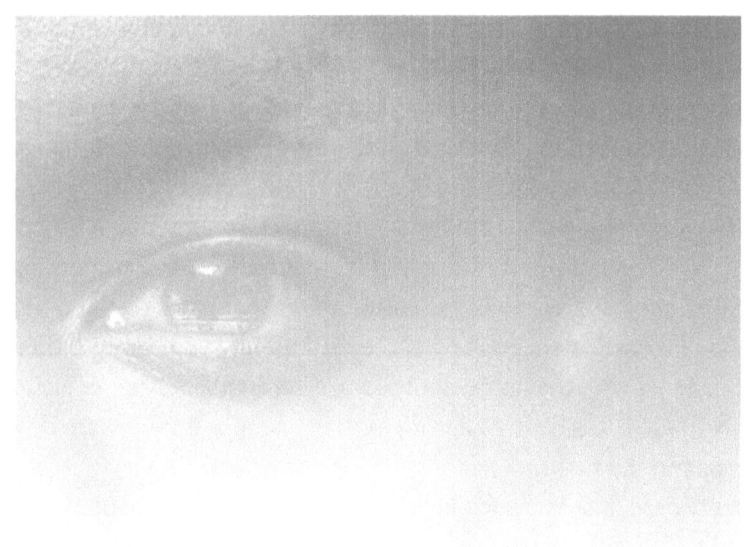

BK. Two letters that might not mean much to many people. But in my generation, they moved mountains; created hate, jealousy, and envy; promoted fear; and produced people both famous and infamous. To the natives, these two letters were loved and represented everywhere and anywhere. You see, BK is more than just two letters—it's where I'm from. Let me take you there.

BK has many different parts to it. You've got Flatbush, East Flatbush, Bed-Stuy, East New York, Brownsville, Fort Greene, Crown Heights, Red Hook, Canarsie, Sunset Park, Bay Ridge, Mill Basin, Howard Beach, Coney Island, Brooklyn Heights, Clinton Hill, Prospect Heights, Downtown Brooklyn, Gowanus, Park Slope, Green Point, Bushwick, Williamsburg, Bensonhurst, Fort Hamilton, New Utrecht, Midwood, Sheepshead Bay, Graves End, Cypress Hill, Highland Park, City Line, Marine Park, and many others. If I didn't mention your specific area, forgive me, but you're probably thought to be part of one that I've mentioned.

As for me, I'm a "Bush baby" born in Kings County Hospital, and I lived there most of my days. Not that I haven't lived in, stomped through, or otherwise made my presence known throughout almost all of BK. But Flatbush is my essence, where the doc smacked me on the ass and the world heard my first cry. Where I got my first piece of pussy, caught my first case, did my first crime, had my first love and my first heartbreak, smoked my first blunt, took my first sip, and fought my first fight—and the first wasn't the last for any of them.

My world began with me being an only child and raised by a single parent. Now, as common as it is today, that wasn't so common back in the 1970s and '80s, especially being the only child. Everybody had at least one brother or sister. And if they didn't have the same father, one of the dads lived in the home with them. And if that brother or sister was older, it made life a little easier for you, especially if they were down or had props in the hood.

In my case, I had no such luck. I was it. I took the brunt of everything life had to offer. If my mom's was having a bad day, there wasn't anyone else around to help absorb her wrath. If I got into beef at school or on the block, there wasn't anyone else to help me fight that battle or watch my back. Even as a little nigga, I knew that I was better off dealing with situations on my own than bringing my mom's to a man's battle. (Well, in those times, a boy's battle.) That was just unheard of. That made you straight-up pussy and would lead you down the road to more problems and a lot more fights. In 1985, I turned twelve years old—and with all that I had endured, I felt like I was already a man. And that's when the real bullshit began.

By the age of twelve, I had been hit with everything that could be swung at me or thrown into my crib, from the iron with which we pressed our clothes to the iron skillet in which we cooked our food—and everything in between that wasn't too big to pick up. I was even awakened from sleep by having hot, hot water thrown on me for something I can't even say that I did. After taking a few beat-downs and giving a few back, I became an angry, aggressive, violent, and extremely lonely child. And when I wasn't on punishment, I was in the street raising all hell.

Around that time I found a couple of pain relievers, weed, and 40s of Olde English malt liquor. I hated cigarettes back then because my mom's smoked them faithfully, and I hated everything about her. But I had made some friends during my journey, a few of whom used to hang out at my junior high school to rob and bully the weaker kids. They had witnessed some of my battles and even helped dish out a couple of my beat-downs 'cause I was fighting one of their little brothers, but this one dude would always be the one breaking things up and sending me on my way home with a mush to the head.

Anyway, one day I was on my way to the store for my mom's and me, and that same dude fell into stride with me. As he exhaled a mouthful of smoke, he said to me, "What's up, little nigga?" Now, because I didn't believe he was actually talking to me, even though there was no one else he could have been talking to, I didn't respond. I guess he got offended by me not replying, so he smacked me in the back of the head as he repeated, "What's up, little nigga?"

This time I replied, "What's up?" All the while, I was hoping that he didn't plan on robbing me of my mom's cigarette and lighter money, which I had balled up in my hand.

He went on to say, "Ain't you that little nigga that I keep saving up at Ditmas?" Out of nowhere, without thought, I began to get angry. It must've showed 'cause he said, "Calm down, little nigga. You damn sure don't want any of this."

So we both entered the store, and from the door he yelled, "Ock, give me two Phillies and a White Owl!" I didn't know what those were or what they were used for, but it kinda looked like what he had been smoking on our way to the store.

As I was asking the man for a pack of Newports and a lighter, I noticed that the dude hadn't left from in front of the store. So now I was getting worried and thinking, *Here we go again.* I prepared myself for a fight, knowing that I'd probably get beat up. He was older and bigger than me, but not by much. I was kinda tall for my age, and me and my friend J Dog were already working out at his house every chance we got when I wasn't on punishment.

To my pleasant surprise, he wasn't looking for a fight. He just fell into stride with me and began to talk as he smoked. He said, "You've got a lot of fight in you, little nigga. That's what's up. How old are you?"

With slight hesitation, I lied and said, "Thirteen."

As he exhaled, he said "Word" and then added, "So how long have you lived out here?" I said, "A while, off and on."

In between coughs, he said, "Off and on? What the fuck does that mean?"

So I explained that I used to live in my building when I was little, and then we had moved away, and now during the summer break we had moved back into the same building.

As he exhaled, he said, "Oh, okay."

As we reached the corner of my block and I turned the corner, he said, "Hold up, little nigga.

Do you know Little T who stays on the corner?"

I replied, "I've met him before." I got another "Word" as he exhaled.

Then he asked a shocking but intriguing question: "Can you come outside?" I hesitated a little too long and got a "Go take ya folks they shit. I'll be right here waiting on ya."

As I departed, I was curious, scared, confused, and nervous all at the same time. Curious to know why this dude was taking interest in me, scared because I didn't know what I'd be getting myself into, confused about what story to tell to get out of the house since no one else was outside yet, and nervous because my mom's might not let me back out. And with him waiting for me, not showing up might cause more problems. As I turned into my building, I looked back at the corner and ... yup, he was still there, looking like a chimney with smoke rising above his head.

As I entered my crib, I faced a moment of truth that would probably make or break me, because fitting into that neighborhood was up to me. Fortunately my mom's was on the phone, having what I guess was a pleasant conversation, because she was smiling and laughing. When I asked if I could go outside, she waved her hand and yelled "Five o'clock!" as I went out the door, which meant I'd better be back in the house by then.

I slowly walked down the two flights of stairs—the longest two flights of stairs ever!—ending at the short corridor that led to the back door of my building. My heart was racing because I had no idea what those next few steps would be getting my ass into. As the sunlight hit me, I was hoping that he wouldn't be there when I turned right to head for the corner. But as my luck would have it, he was still there—along with another dude slightly taller than him, both of them looking like chimney stacks with smoke rising above their heads.

My heart began to beat even faster at that sight. It was one thing to deal with the dude who seemed like he was cool so far, but this new dude? My mind was racing as my feet kept moving me closer. *What if it's a setup to beat me down? What am I getting myself into? Can I outrun these niggas and make it to the front door where the doorman is?*

Just as my nerves were getting the best of me, I heard, "Come on, little nigga. Shit, it took you long enough."

All I can remember thinking was that I hoped I made it home.

As I got closer to the two dudes, the one who had gotten me into that predicament asked the other, "You know this little nigga?"

The other dude said, "Naw, I don't know that nigga."

The first guy then said, "Remember the fight up at the school on Monday? When J Rock's little brother was getting his ass kicked by another little nigga till we jumped in? And niggas were mad at me for breaking it up before niggas could punish him?"

The second guy said, "Oh, hell yeah, you bitch ass!"

The dude that had me there then said, "This is the little nigga that was kicking J Rock's brother's ass."

The second dude replied, "Oh shit. Okay, what's up, little nigga?" I responded, "What's up?"

He then asked my name, but before I could answer, he introduced himself. "I'm Bone Breaker —BB for short."

After a brief pause, I said, "I'm Leroy."

BB cracked a joke to his boy, who had been invited to hang with him like in *The Last Dragon*. He repeated my name in his imitation of Sho'nuff—"Leroy!"—and began to laugh and cough at the same time. Then he added, "Yo, Screw, what the fuck are you doing with this little nigga?"

As BB continued laughing, Screw replied, "I like the little nigga. He's got fight in him," and then he settled down from his laughing and smoking.

BB then said, "Yeah, he sure does. He would've beat the shit out of J Rock's brother if niggas didn't step in." They gave each other daps of agreement about that fact.

I chimed in, "I sure would've bit—"

BB cut me off and said, "Hooo, don't get cocky, Leroy," in his Sho'nuff voice again, and we all stood there laughing for a minute.

In between coughs, Screw said, "Shit, all this shit's made me thirsty. Let's go to the store." When we got to the store, Screw told BB, "Give me a dollar."

As Screw entered the store, I stayed outside because I didn't have any money, even though I was thirsty too.

BB stayed with me, I guess for company and to kick it a bit while Screw was gone. He looked at me and said, "So you like to rumble, huh, little nigga? I've seen you in a couple throw downs up at the school."

I said, "Naw, not really. But niggas keep fucking with me 'cause they think I'm the new herb on the block."

BB replied, "I feel you, little nigga. Can't have niggas trying to play you for pussy out here. It'll make your days long and painful. You're doing the right thing. But don't sweat it, 'cause we've got ya back. That means the whole crew has got ya back, and you won't be getting fucked with anymore. Trust and believe that." He gave me a dap as confirmation of that fact, and then he began imitating Sho'nuff again—"Leroy"—and acting like he was doing karate. I didn't know that BB was high as a kite—or even what it felt like to be high, but I was definitely about to find out.

Screw came out of the store and we all began to walk Argyle toward Dorchester. As we were walking, both Screw and BB fired up their half-smoked blunts.

My curiosity was killing me, so I asked, "Hey, what y'all smoking?" It sure as hell didn't look or smell like the cigarettes my mom's smoked. The sidewalks couldn't fit three dudes across, so I was walking close behind him.

BB glanced over his shoulder at me and said, "That boom bonic. You ain't ready for all this yet, Leroy," in his Sho'nuff voice. The joke was on me, but them two niggas were laughing like Richard Pryor was walking with us.

Wanting to be down, I insisted, "Let me try it." Boy, I had no idea what I was in for. Screw threw BB an elbow and said, "Let the little nigga hit it."

BB replied, "Let his ass hit your blunt. Shit, you're the one who got him hanging with us."

Screw said, "Shit, I will" as he passed me the blunt. We'd almost reached the corner, and we all stopped. Screw then said, "Take ya time, little nigga. Don't go and blow your chest out ya body."

The first pull made me cough uncontrollably. When I stopped coughing, my head felt like it was about to start hurting, but that subsided quickly. The next pull went a bit more smoothly. I began to feel something, but I didn't know what was happening to me.

Before I could take a third pull, Screw snatched his blunt and said, "Take ya time, little nigga.

You've got to crawl before you can walk."

I didn't understand that statement then, but soon it became perfectly clear. We began walking again, making a left at the corner heading toward Ocean Avenue. I started to feel heavy, and there was like a delay between the words coming out of Screw's mouth and me actually hearing what he was saying.

"Are you okay, little nigga? Are you okay?" Screw kept asking me.

I was saying "Yeah," but I wasn't quite feeling okay. Just when I thought I couldn't walk any farther, we took a seat on some steps. Now, I knew that neighborhood pretty well. On my block, when we weren't playing round-up or tag, my boy J Dog and I would ride around breaking the pots of flowers people had in front of their cribs, speeding away laughing so as not to get caught being mischievous little kids. But for the life of me, I couldn't tell you where I was at that moment. I knew I was there, but I couldn't have told you where. All I knew was that Screw and BB were getting a kick out of the predicament I had put myself in.

The last thing I remember before being shaken was Screw handing BB a bag with something to drink in it. BB tapped it twice and then handed it back to Screw. Boy, was I thirsty! I didn't know what all the tapping was about. I thought they would share, 'cause I was thirsty as hell. Next thing I knew, Sho'nuff was calling my name and laughing as he shook me back to alertness. As my vision regained focus, I could see BB in my face with a big-ass grin, asking if I was okay. All I could do was smile back at him. Off to BB's left, Screw was laughing like he had just heard the funniest shit in the world.

I just knew that I was thirsty and needed something to drink. I kept thinking it, and finally I found the voice to say it: "Give me something to drink. My mouth is drier than a motherfucker." That made them both laugh like hell, but then they passed me what felt like a two-liter of soda but in a bottle. The taste was a lot harsher than soda on my throat and tongue, but I didn't care. It was ridding me of my cotton mouth, and that was the mission at hand. Little did I know that I was drinking Olde English, which was about to make my situation a lot worse before it got any better.

Screw finally snatched the forty ounce from me, yelling at BB, "Yo, why you letting that nigga drink all that fucking beer?"

BB yelled back, "The nigga thirsty!" as he laughed at my ignorance.

"Well, your ass gonna make sure that nigga makes it home," Screw yelled back.

"This ain't no day care center," BB threw back at him, "and if his little grown ass can't make it, his ass will stay right here."

Even through the high from the beer and marijuana, I began to understand the situation before me, and I knew that I had to get home. I tried to stand, but my legs wouldn't cooperate. When my ass hit those concrete steps, it was like falling off a building. I rolled off those steps and hit the sidewalk. I knew that I was in serious trouble, and I didn't have a clue how to get myself out of that one. All I could think about was my mom's kicking my ass for not making it into the house by curfew. Somehow I began to fight the feeling and found the strength to get to my feet.

I don't know whether it was the thought of my mom's kicking my ass, those two fake-ass comedians in the background cracking jokes about a nigga and laughing their asses off, or just divine intervention, but somehow I made it to my feet. Through blurry eyes and on wobbly legs, I began walking my ass home with these two asshole niggas in tow, laughing their asses off, saying shit like, "I think I can, I think I can." Every so often I'd stumble and fall to a knee or completely, and I'd hear, "Aww, poor baby go boom."

As fucked as I was, I was angry and wanted to fight, but I was in no condition for any battle other than getting my ass home. I did manage to yell a wholehearted "Fuck you!" every now and again, but that seemed to tickle them even more—which made me even angrier and further drove me to make it home.

As I bent the corner of my block, I knew it was almost over. *Just a few more steps*, I told myself. *Shit, I think I can, I think I can.* At my building, the doorman opened the door and I heard him ask, "Are you okay?" but I didn't reply. I was in the home stretch. *Just a little bit farther.* Going up the stairs was a no-no, but all of my effort was almost for no good because I passed out on my feet waiting for the elevator. The sound of the elevator door closing brought me back, however, and I pushed the button and waited for it again. If I had fallen out of the elevator and added "embarrassing my mom's" to the equation, I'd really have been done for.

As I reached my door, I gathered myself, located my key, and entered my crib. God truly poured his grace on me, because I could hear my mom's in the shower. Even though I made it home an hour and change before curfew, I knew she would've killed me if she had seen the condition I was in. I went straight to my room, got out of my clothes, and fell dead asleep.

My mom's didn't know that I had entered our crib, and she didn't even think to look in my room before she ran out of the crib in a fury at five o'clock. The doorman must've been on a break as my furious mother stormed out of the building looking for me. She went to the cribs of all my friends on the block and came up empty. Finally, after two hours of searching the neighborhood, she returned to the building—angry as hell, but also worried enough to call the police. She asked the doorman, "Have you seen my child?"

He said, "Yeah, about four hours ago, and he—."

Before he could say anything and add insult to injury, she stormed away and headed to our crib. Instead of feeling relieved, she got even angrier, so she went to the kitchen and began to boil some water. Right as it bubbled its first bubble, she took the pot and headed to my room. I can only imagine the burns that I would've suffered if I hadn't been under a blanket.

I was awake then—and as sober as a motherfucker. I felt lost and didn't know what had just happened or why. She was gone, and the only things there were a hot pot and a pair of oven mitts. I became angry and felt like a demon was brewing inside me. I wanted so bad to hurt that woman. I couldn't, because she was my mother, but the world would feel my pain.

My mother went to work the next day, but I was too caught up in my feelings to sneak outside anyway. Unless she was pulling some overtime, she worked twelve-hour shifts—9:00 a.m. to 9:00 p.m.—four days a week, with Thursdays, Fridays, and Saturdays off. So on school days, I basically parented myself and did what I felt like, which was part of the reason why I found myself getting so many ass whippings and being punished so much. But I was used to it, and when she dished it out, I'd take it like the G she was making me into.

I didn't sneak outside on Sunday, because I was going through it mentally as well as physically, so I didn't have the opportunity to see anybody. That Monday morning rolled around good before I stole from my first victim, which wasn't their fault. I wasn't paying attention to them as I tried to bend the corner headed for school, which was only four blocks from my crib. We bumped into each other, and before he could say a word, I hit his ass so hard that it seemed like he almost came out of his shoes. Kids came running out like there was gonna be a fight, but there wasn't one. A kid just got knocked out, and I kept it pushing.

There was a bicycle store on that same corner, where the super of my building would be chilling with one of his friends who owned the shop. He saw the altercation, but at the time I didn't know or care who saw what I did. At the same time, the neighborhood crew was doing what they did—robbing people. They were kind of deep, about twenty-five of them, give or take a couple. They stayed in small bunches, three to five of them at different spots on Cortelyou Road. One group was at the train station beating and robbing the same man, and another bunch was on Coney Island Avenue doing the same thing.

But I wasn't aware of any of that, so when I heard police sirens and saw cars flying around, I thought they were looking for me. I cut up Stratford and took off running, slamming straight into a dude I shared a couple of classes with named G-baby. He slowed me down to find out what was going on, and I told him, "I just knocked some kid out around the corner, and I think the po- po is after me."

It just so happened that we were in front of his yard, so he told me, "Stay here and keep low." Then he went to see what was going on. After about twenty minutes, which felt like two hours, he returned to tell me that it wasn't me they were looking for. Instead, they were searching for the culprits who had robbed a couple of people.

So me and G-baby were headed toward school when we bumped into Screw, BB, and about five other dudes I didn't know. Immediately Screw and BB burst out laughing and filling in their boys on what had gone down with me on Saturday. Everybody started laughing at me, which caused my anger to return.

I let out a "Fuck you" as I continued walking, and immediately the five dudes I didn't know tried to surround me. But before anything could jump off, BB told his boys to chill. "That's my little nigga Leroy" he said in his Sho'nuff voice. Four of the dudes had no problem letting the shit die, but a dude BB called Billy stayed in my path. BB had to call this nigga twice while we were screwing each other, with neither of us afraid or ready to back down.

As Billy walked past me, he bumped my shoulder. I spun with it, catching him on the back of his head with a right that sent him face-first into the pavement. The shit happened so fast that I amazed my damn self. Before the others could pounce, BB and Screw were between us. BB yelled at his boys to chill and told G-baby to get me to school. Everybody knew G-baby and his uncle Hulk, and nobody wanted any problems with them.

But at the time, I didn't know any of that. All I knew was that I wanted to get at the one they called Billy, and Billy definitely wanted to get at me. All the way up the block and around the corner, I could hear him screaming, "I'm gonna see you, son. I'm gonna see you, son."

As we were entering the school, G-baby told me that little Billy Bad Ass, as his full name went, was the youngest of three brothers, who were flip a lot for short FA which was BB and Screw's age, and their oldest brother, Scream, was up north doing a seven-and-a-half to fifteen. G-baby said that I'd better stay on point, 'cause those dudes were trouble with a capital T. But as we entered our homeroom class, he expressed his appreciation for the way I had touched Billy's bad ass back there, giving me a dap to confirm that fact. I just smiled slightly.

While we were in school, things on the streets were going like they did basically every day. But when you're not there, you wouldn't know unless you watched the news or fell victim to something. Billy, with his bad ass, was so enraged by being put down by a virtual unknown that he jumped the gun, tried to set it on an undercover cop, and got locked up.

G-baby's uncle Hulk was a drug dealer. Drug beef was the only time guns really came into play. I'm not saying niggas weren't dropping, but it was rare for a crew or posse beef to get handled with a gun. Niggas usually died from a knife wound or just straight up got beat to death with some blunt object. But as time passed, more guns were hitting the streets, and now innocent people were getting hurt or killed because of inexperienced gun handlers. Hulk was a straight-up G and a drug dealer who met his demise in a robbery at one of his spots in Brownsville.

Now I'm gonna keep it 100. Back in the day, places like Bed-Stuy, Brownsville, and Crown Heights were doing shit different from Flatbush. There were a lot more drug spots and beef in those places, so there were a lot more niggas dying from guns in those places.

Back to the Bush. By the time three o'clock hit, G-baby had lost an uncle but didn't know it yet. Billy was knocked. The police were looking for Screw because his was the only other description the cop could pick out of the mug shots. Only eighteen, Screw was one of the few from our immediate crew who ever had to do real time in prison. He finally had to do a year and a half for robbery after his third time being caught and getting probation. The system had had their fill of Screw, and if they caught him this time, he'd be headed up north.

When three o'clock came, we exited the school. The crowd on the corner was a lot larger than usual. As I got closer, the only familiar face I saw was this kid Johnny from science class. Johnny was from Parkside, and the word brewing on the streets was that he'd been robbed by Billy and the crew the previous week. The crew on the corner was Johnny's regular crew, Billy's crew was late because of the day's events, which happened from time to time. *Shit, I thought, what a day for these niggas to be late.*

Before I could take another step, G-baby grabbed my shoulder from behind and said, "Slow down. It's about to go down out here. Johnny and his boys are looking for Billy and them."

I asked, "Where them niggas at?"

He said, "I don't know, but let's wait right here for a second. The crew isn't going to disappoint them niggas." As he said that, the crowd on the corner turned around and started moving toward Coney Island Avenue.

G-baby said, "They're here," in a funny yet eerie tone. He then pulled on my shoulder and said, "Come on."

As we reached the corner, I wasn't exactly prepared for what I was about to see. Apparently the crew did show up, and it was on. There was fighting everywhere, in the middle of the street and on both sidewalks. The fight was so crazy that it stopped traffic. There were fights on people's cars with the people yelling out the windows, "Get the fuck off my car!" It was straight pandemonium out there.

G-baby told me, "Stay close, and if a nigga get close, hit 'em." No sooner had he said that than some dude came straight for us. Before I could react, G-baby hit that nigga, but he didn't fall. He kept coming, so I hit him and G-baby hit him again, which sent the dude to the ground. G-baby began to kick and stomp on him, and I joined in.

From nowhere, I felt something or someone hit me in the back of the head, and I went flying into a parked car. G-baby turned just in time to dip a blow that might've put him out, and then he kicked the dude in the dick. Coming off the car, I dropped an elbow to the back of the dude's neck since he was bending over, but G-baby was giving him a knee to the face. We both caught the dude at the same time, which put that dude down.

My adrenaline was pumping. I looked across the street and saw Screw getting into it with two dudes. Without a thought, I was across the street with my book bag in hand. As I got closer, I swung it and caught one dude on the side of the head just as Screw was giving the other dude a two piece that made the two dudes slam into each other.

Like we were Siamese twins, Screw and I both swung on the two dudes, putting them on the ground.

Then I wondered, *Where's G?* Looking around, I caught a glimpse of him being jumped by two dudes. I tugged on Screw's sleeve to follow one of the two dudes that had G-baby for a second. Shit was crazy. Can you imagine like sixty kids just rumbling in the street? Our crew was outnumbered by like fifteen, but you couldn't tell because we were handling ours. Screw turned to his left, but before G and I could follow, we had two more dudes on us. We gave them the business, though, and then gave each other a dap after they hit the ground.

But through the commotion, you could hear the sirens getting closer. G tugged on my arm for me to follow him, and we started running down East Ninth. We busted a left at the corner,

crossed Coney Island Avenue, and finally—tired and out of breath—reached G-baby's crib.

When this nigga was able to speak, all I could say was "That shit there was crazy" between my heaves.

G-baby replied, "Hell, yeah—but fun!" We smiled and gave each other daps.

Meanwhile, the Ville was in an uproar over Hulk being killed. Hulk had been an icon to those niggas out there. He had made sure niggas had food on the table, the freshest wears to go to school, money to pay the rent—like a regular fucking Robinhood.

Spider, Hulk's brother, was flipping on Dropout and Spaz, his cousins, who were the lieutenants and head of security. "How the fuck could you dickhead niggas let this happen? How the fuck did these niggas even get close to this nigga? That's my fucking brother and your fucking cousin out there dead, son. How the fuck?"

Before Spaz could get the words out of his mouth, Spider punched him in the face, sending him back a couple of steps. Spider looked at his fist, then at his cousin, and thought, *Damn, I'm getting old. I used to knock a nigga out no matter how big they were.*

Spaz was a big dude, six foot three and 230 pounds, and had just done eight and a half up north. He was ready to spaz out, but Spider was his cousin. And Spaz understood, 'cause Spider's brother, their lifeline, had just been killed.

Spider asked, "Yo, Dropout, what the fuck happened?"

"I don't know," said Dropout. "I was in the back with Spaz, getting the bread ready for Hulk. All I know is Hulk came in, we dapped, and he said, 'Go get that paper.' Murph was on the door. Next thing I heard was two shots, then another. Spaz and I were headed from the living room. Hulk was falling to the couch and managed to squeeze off two shots, hitting the nigga closest to him. The other two niggas had seen us coming and were headed back out the door as I emptied at them."

Spaz jumped in and said, "I ran out of the building after them niggas and put four into the back of a black Jeep with Jersey plates. I swear I hit one. That's my word. When I went back inside, Murph was dead and Drop was telling Hulk to hold on."

Drop jumped back in and said, "I was holding him, son. He was coughing up blood and said, 'You better kill them motherfuckers,' and that was it. He was gone. I yelled at Spaz to go get the shit. Then we jetted to the stash crib on the third floor, stashed the money and drugs, went out the back window and down the fire escape, and came to the crib and called you. That's my word."

"Murph wouldn't have opened the door for just anybody with Hulk at the spot," said Spaz. "He knew better than that. It had to have been somebody important. They had to have known they could get in."

"What-the-fuck-ever," Spider said. "Let me think." Spider had a million things running through his head as he paced back and forth, trying to control the rage in his heart. "Yo, did you recognize any of them? The one Hulk shot? Anybody?"

They both said, "Naw, son." Drop added that the three dudes had been wearing ski masks. "I didn't think to stop and pull the shit off."

"*Fuck*," Spider yelled. "What the fuck am I going to tell Killa?" Then he damn near whispered, "What the fuck am I going to tell him?"

Hulk had three boys and two girls. Killa, the oldest, was one of the meanest motherfuckers out there, and he was due home in a week from doing four joints up north. Only twenty-two, Killa was just as big as Spaz—six foot one, 222 pounds—and a loose cannon, to say the least. He wasn't going to take his pop's being murdered very well.

Lost in thought, Spider fell into a chair. "I'm glad that nigga wasn't here or even free. He might've smoked them two knuckleheads over there. Shit, he still might, if we don't have some answers or blood by the time he gets home."

Spider came out of his trance, jumped up and got in Drop's face, and said in a sinister tone, "You motherfuckers better get out there and find out who did this, who's behind it." Then he yelled, with spit coming out of his mouth, "Get me some fucking info."

As Spaz and Dropout left, Spider fell back into the chair feeling drained, mind racing, trying to figure out who could have done it. Thinking about Killa reminded him of his own son, Deuce, who was Killa's cousin and best friend. Deuce had been with Killa the night that robbery had gone down, but they had split up. Deuce had seen the number of police and thought to stash the guns and money in some alley. Even though they both got picked up, they had pistol-whipped the dude so bad that he had ID'd only Killa's ass in the lineup, and Killa hadn't snitched on Deuce.

Spider knew that when those two were reunited, even if it wasn't the motherfuckers responsible for Hulk's death, blood was definitely going to be shed. "Shit is going to get hectic," Spider said aloud, to nobody but himself.

Deuce lived with his little sister, in the East on a side block right outside Cypress Projects, in a crib that his pop's had got for his mom's. His mom's had passed three years earlier, murdered for some shit that either Deuce or his pop's had done. The killer had left a note in his mom's mouth that said, "You're next, bitch." Deuce took care of his sister with financial help from his pop's— that's it.

Deuce became a different dude after his mom's was killed. He had been wild before it happened, but that shit—along with all the woos he was smoking on a daily basis—made him even wilder. Although Deuce was two years older, Killa was about twenty pounds heavier and three inches taller, and Killa liked to playfully push his cousin around. They were each other's heart, more like brothers than cousins.

Deuce was coming in the crib, from shopping on the Pitkin and City line for him and Killa, when he heard his sister crying. He immediately dropped the bags and pulled out his chrome .32 with the ivory handle, which went everywhere with him. Slowly moving through the crib, he made sure every room was clear. When he found his sister sitting on the couch, he holla'd at her, "Yo, what's up?"

She jumped up and ran to him screaming, "Uncle H is dead!"

Deuce stood there in shock, holding his crying sister and trying to swallow the bomb that had just been dropped on him. He couldn't imagine that anyone would kill Uncle Hulk. *Naw, that's impossible*, he thought. *Shit, it's been years since they did anybody dirty. I was the driver on their last job. They didn't need to violate anyone after that, at least not directly.*

Anger began to fill his veins, pumping his heart full of venom. He pushed his sister and told her to chill, then stormed back down the hall, grabbed the bags sitting by the front door, and went to his bedroom. Rolling his blunt, he thought, *Damn, I was just with him this morning. Uncle H had just dropped off ten pounds of weed, a half brick of coke, and a sixty-two of dope. I can remember the last words he said to me as he got into a fresh L dog: "Be careful out here, nephew."*

"Naw, that nigga can't be dead!" he yelled out loud. Putting the finishing touches on a fat coke-laced blunt, he left his bedroom and headed for the front door. He was fuming and barely heard his sister scream "Trey!" as the door slammed shut behind him.

Deuce stayed on the main level, but his two lieutenants and their two lieutenants rented the two apartments on the second and third floors. When he got to the second floor and used his key to enter the apartment, he became even angrier at the filth those niggas had. No one was there, so he went to the third floor and entered. Lil' Mook was in the process of cleaning, so their shit looked a little better. Deuce yelled, "Yo, drop that broom and go get CC, Dino, and Batman. Oh, and tell them to bring Stick with them."

Lil' Mook could tell by the rage on the boss man's face that this shit was serious, so he didn't hesitate to do what he was told. Fuck what Batman had said about how the crib had better be clean by the time he got back. The big boss had given an order, and Lil' Mook knew that he had better listen. All the way to the P's, Lil' Mook was hoping it wasn't something that he had fucked up that made Deuce look like that. The last time he had seen Deuce that angry, that nigga Trigger was doing laps in the courtyard butt naked before Deuce finally put two in his naked body. Lil' Mook was hoping none of them were next, especially not himself.

He didn't even have to go into the P's, because everybody except CC was right on the corner.

As Lil' Mook ran up to them, Batman said, "Nigga, I hope that—"

But Lil' Mook cut him off, saying, "Yo, Deuce wants us at the crib right now. And he's madder than a motherfucker, son."

Dino was like, "What the fuck we done did now?"

Then Lil' Mook asked, "Where's CC? And Stick, he wants you too." Dino said, "I sent him on a mission. He'll be back in a few."

Everybody looked at Stick, who said, "Shit, I ain't do nothing. I don't even touch shit. I'm just out here holding y'all niggas down, making sure nobody gets the drop on us. Don't fucking look at me."

They were all worried and nervous as they headed to the crib. Dino yelled back at Meathead, "Tell CC to come to the crib when he gets back." They knew Deuce could get on some bullshit when he was high off that woo shit. They were the only ones who knew Deuce smoked that shit, and none of them wanted to be the victim of one of his too-high fits.

When they got back to Batman and Lil' Mook's crib, it stank bad of Deuce's woo blunt. Batman looked at the others and said, "Damn, here we go." When they entered the living room and saw Deuce, it shocked and really scared the shit out of them. None of them were pussy, but they had never seen anything like that.

Deuce was sitting on the couch with tears flowing from his bloodshot eyes, a shotie on either side of him, and his trusty .32 in his lap. "Don't just fucking stand there. Sit the fuck down," he told them.

Batman spoke first and asked, "What's happenin', Captain?" After a long pull, Deuce replied, "They've killed my uncle Hulk."

Stick had never met Hulk, but the others were immediately bothered by the news. Each of them had been blessed by Hulk at least once with a grand or two, a pound of weed, a half ounce of dope, and so on. He would just roll up, tell you to get in, and before he let you out of the car —*Bam!* He'd give you something and say, "That's for you. Take care of my nephew out here or the first one's for you." And he'd point to the big-ass Colt .45 that he kept in his lap.

Batman even started to shed a tear as he stood and asked, "What's good? Who do we have to kill?"

Deuce said, "Chill for now. We're gonna go check my pop's, if he doesn't make it over here first." He reached in his pocket, pulled out a wad of cash, and said to Stick, "Go get as many Ballantine Ales as this will buy."

But Batman said, "Naw, son, I got this," and handed Stick a fifty-dollar bill. They all knew that Hulk had looked out for them niggas, but Batman felt like Hulk had been his uncle too. Shit, even more than that. Hulk used to slide by his crib every now and then to fuck his mom's, and he had taken very good care of her. Batman's family had never wanted for anything.

All that shit was going to change now. Batman was just as fucked up about the news as Deuce was, and to make shit even worse, he had to tell his mom's. He knew she wasn't going to take that news well. Batman even believed that his eleven-year-old brother was Hulk's son. His mom's had never confirmed it, but no other niggas ever came to his mom's crib while Batman lived there—or since he had moved out. He would know, because they lived four houses down. Batman had nothing but respect for Hulk, and if it was up to him, he'd put a clip full in the motherfucker or motherfuckers personally. He also knew that Killa and that crazy nigga was coming next week, so he might not get the opportunity.

Deuce told Batman to go and get the weed he had stashed. It was time to get high. They kept a box of Phillies on the table, so when Batman returned, he dropped about a pound on the table. Then he dropped $750 on Deuce's lap and said, "That's for the weed, my nigga." As fucked up as Deuce was, that gesture made him crack a smile and reach to give Batman a dap. Batman grabbed Deuce's wrist, pulled him to his feet, and gave his Ace a hug. Who says killers have no heart?

"Yooo, I'm hit, star," said the gunman in the back seat. "Where, dread?" asked the other passenger.

"Me shoulder, to ras," he said. "Just cool," said the driver.

"Wha ta blood clot cool," he responded. "Drive dis bomb clot car, star."

All the driver could hear was the don's orders: "Don't bring me back no fuckery." So the three hit men were flying through Brownsville and up Rockaway, trying to catch the lights but not running any so as not to get pulled by the police.

"Ee watch da police, boy. Dem coming up on de lef. Slow down, dread." The driver took his foot off the gas as the car came toward them, but the police were headed to the crime scene, so they weren't really paying any mind to the speeding Jeep.

"Hol' tight, breddrin. Me gon get cha deer. Hol' tight," the driver said. He made a left on Atlantic, then a right onto Marcus Garvey. He finally slowed down and looked around as he slid into a parking spot. A few people were around, but no police. The driver then turned around and asked, "Yah good, breddrin?"

"Yeah, mon," said the gunman in the back seat.

Pow! One shot.

The startled passenger asked, "Wha de bomba?"

"Me can't bring dis mon back to de don," the gunman explained, exiting the vehicle. "Come on." At the corner, another car waited to carry them to Crown Heights, where the don was waiting.

Chilling in the yard, we had just finished smoking G-baby's clip when he noticed his mom's car turning into the driveway to their garage. "Oh shit, my mom's 'Straighten up, son. Don't look so high.'"

Turning to his mom, G-baby said, "Hey, Ma, you're home early. This is Leroy. He lives around the corner and goes to school with me."

"Hello, Leroy. Gerald, I need to see you inside," she replied. "Tell your friend you'll see him later."

"Later, son," G-baby said to me as we gave each other dap, and I left the yard. As G-baby entered his crib, all I could think was, *I hope he's not in trouble*. Even though I was higher than a kite, I could see on her face that something was seriously wrong.

As I entered my building, the doorman opened the door shaking his head and said, "I'm glad to see you're still alive."

I glanced at him and just said, "Yeah," as I made my way to my crib. I was glad my mom's wasn't home, 'cause she would've had a fit if she had seen my new jacket torn and me with no book bag. As I tried my best to patch up my jacket, I began to get hungrier than a motherfucker. So I went into the kitchen and warmed up some leftovers, which tasted better than they had the night before.

I was really tired, so as soon as I finished eating, I put my dishes in the sink and went to bed. When my mom's came home, she was surprised to see me knocked out in the bed. She took her shower and turned on the TV to watch the news, but she fell asleep as the reporter was talking about three more people dead on Dumont Avenue.

When G-baby went inside his crib, his mother told him to have a seat. He was wondering what he had done to deserve a talking to, but the first few words out of her mouth blew his mind.

"Your uncle Biron is dead."

"Stop playing, Ma. That's impossible," G-baby said.

"This is why I tell you to take your ass to school, get a good education, and stay out of them streets."

G-baby was in a daze and didn't even hear what his mother was saying. He just couldn't accept that somebody had killed the mighty Hulk. He had thought that his uncle was invincible. "Are you serious, Ma?"

"As a heart attack, son. You see, even strong men can fall victim to these streets, and they're just getting worse. I need you to promise me that you'll stay out of these godforsaken streets, Gerald."

G-baby took too long to respond, and his mother yelled, "Promise me, damn it!" "Okay, Ma, I promise."

She pulled him out of the chair and hugged him tight. "I don't know what I'd do if I was to lose you, Gerald."

The next morning, I woke up earlier than usual. I guess it was because that weed had knocked me out earlier than usual the previous night. I was eager to get out of the house—not to get to school, but to avoid my mom's seeing that I didn't have my book bag and my jacket was torn. By the time my mom's was up, I was showered, dressed, and ready to go—moving so fast that she didn't have time to get her bearings and ask me anything. I was out the door with a "See you later, Ma."

As I left the building, she caught me off guard by yelling, "Did you eat breakfast, boy?" I said, "Yes, Ma," and kept it moving.

My route changed that morning so that I could link up with G-baby and go to school with him, but it seemed like he was running late. When I reached his crib, I just yelled, because I didn't know which window was his. I was caught off guard when his mom's came to the door and said Gerald wasn't going to school.

"Morning, ma'am. Okay," I said, and went on my way, wondering what was wrong with G- baby. *Oh well*, I thought as I walked down Coney Island Avenue toward Cortelyou Road. I crossed the street before I reached the corner, so Screw and them didn't see me coming. As I bent the corner, they were talking about the rumble that had happened the previous day at school.

BB spotted me first and said, "There's ya boy now, Screw."

Screw had his back to me, but he spun around with a fake playful blow. "My nigga," he said as he grabbed me, then let me go for dap. "Where's G-baby?" he asked.

"He's not coming," I said.

"Cool, little nigga. You ever cut school, little nigga?" "Naw," I replied.

"Well, today's your day," Screw said.

"Okay," I said, but I wasn't in complete agreement with that decision. I knew that it would cause an ass whipping if my mom's found out, but how could I say no? I was being accepted, and acceptance was better than harassment as far as I was concerned.

The usual dudes were there except Billy, and Screw proceeded with introductions. "Yo, Little, Spank, Boy Boy, Trouble, this is Leroy," he said in his Sho'nuff voice. I was about tired of that shit, and we must've been thinking the same thing at the same time. "We've got to get you a name, little nigga," he said.

I was like, "How's L?"

Screw stood there like he was thinking and said, "I guess that'll do for now. But when you meet Big L, he might not agree."

I thought, *Who's Big L?*

And again, he must've been reading my mind. "We'll probably see him before the day is over."

Little did I know that it wasn't going to be just my first day of cutting school. There would be a couple more firsts and a lot more people to meet.

We chilled on the corner until the final school bell rang, and then we proceeded down Cortelyou Road toward the train station. Along the way, niggas were joking and planning the day, and we picked up a few more dudes. When we reached the store, two dudes were chilling and having their own conversation. Everybody else was giving each other dap, and when the two dudes got to me, they were like, "Who's this nigga?"

"I'm L," I replied.

Screw jumped in, "That's my little nigga L. L, that's Nut and Drama." They gave me a dap. BB was like, "Who's got ends on the Forties?"

Niggas were broke for real. Everybody scraped up what they had. When BB looked at me, I said, "I'm tapped out."

"Broke-ass niggas," BB said as he entered the store alone.

While BB was inside, Drama asked, "Was niggas going to Shontay's hookie party?"

Screw was like, "Hell yeah, she knows mad bitches. She goes to Clara Barton, and ain't nothing but bitches up in there. That shit should be off the hook."

At that moment, BB came out carrying a shopping bag with four 40s in it. "Broke motherfuckers," he said, "I know the first thing niggas is doing is catching a pocket or two."

I stood there thinking, *Hookie party? Catching a pocket or two? What the hell have I gotten myself into?*

BB then took out a 40 and said, "Y'all niggas can share them. This here is mines." I didn't care, but the others didn't seem too happy about sharing three 40s between eight niggas.

Snatching a 40 out of the bag, Screw said, "Shit, we most definitely got to catch a healthy pocket before we go to the party. I ain't got but one blunt, and I damn sure ain't gonna get high with nine niggas on it. Yo, L, carry the bag."

We proceeded toward the train station. When we got there, I saw Little T sitting on a dumpster smoking a blunt by himself. He jumped down as niggas approached and began dapping everybody. When he reached me, he smiled and said, "So you found your way off the block, huh?"

"Yeah," I said.

"Hope you're ready. Smoke?" he said, handing the blunt to me. "What type shit is that, passing the blunt to him first?" Screw asked.

"It's my shit, and I can pass it to whoever the fuck I want," Little T replied. Screw said, "Watch ya mouth, motherfucker."

"Make me," Little T said, and they begin sparring right there.

Now I was still new to all that, so I thought it was serious, but they were slapping each other instead of punching. I soon found out that was normal behavior among the crew—in fact, it was mandatory. If you let any crew member punk you, being in the crew wouldn't be fun at all. They would punk you until you manned up and got the best of a few niggas, and you'd sure better not let anyone outside the crew play you without a fight. You'd get treated like you weren't down, and you'd end up with anything from an ass whipping to everybody taking everything you had. Those were lessons I learned quickly.

When Screw and Little T were finished slapping each other, they dapped and hugged. It was over.

BB said, "Yo, T, what are you doing out here so early by yourself?"

"The early bird catches the worm," Little T replied. "Smoked my last blunt last night. I need my shit for today. I've been all the way to Flatbush and the weed spot already."

BB dapped him and said, "I know that's right."

"Where the fuck y'all going?" Little T asked.

"We're about to hop on the train and see what we can catch before we head to Shontay's party," answered BB.

"Word," said Little T. "Shontay's having a party? I'm rolling."

Spank went into the train station to see if the coast was clear. When he whistled, we walked through the gate without paying. The token booth clerk yelled through the loudspeaker, "Pay your fare!" and got a "Fuck you" in unison as a reply.

Little T said, "We're better off going toward Manhattan. There are more herbs that way." And so we went.

For me, this was all new and—I'll admit—kind of exciting. I just hoped that it didn't lead to me getting into trouble with my mom's. Niggas were hyped and getting drunk rapidly. They were down to their last 40, and we weren't even on the train yet. I was glad, because I was getting tired of holding that bag. As train approached, my anxiety was growing. I really didn't know what to expect, but I just kept telling myself to stay alert. Because of everyone's greed, no one noticed I wasn't drinking. Even though the weed had me high, I was handling it like a soldier.

When the train came to a stop, the doors opened and a few people got off. That's when the real excitement started. We were all underage and should have been in school, so after ten o'clock in the morning, we had to avoid the police—whether we had done something to someone or not. If they caught us, they'd hold us for the truancy cops, and our parents would definitely be notified before we were released. Besides that, we weren't the only group of kids riding the trains and looking for trouble. We never knew who or what we'd run into, as I would soon learn firsthand.

The doors closed and "Next stop, Beverly Road" was announced over the intercom. Things were uneventful until we reached Atlantic Avenue, where the 2, 3, 4, 5, B, Q, N, R, and Long Island trains all met—which meant a lot of people, a lot of crews, and a lot of herbs.

BB said, "Let's get off here." Little T agreed, and we all exited the train.

Little T came up to me and said, "I hope you're as fast here as you are on the block. Stay close to me, okay? Shit's about to get hectic."

I didn't understand, but I listened. The next thing I knew, I heard a scream, then another, and yet another. The crew had sprung into action, and I was standing there holding a bag with a 40 in it. "Come on," I heard as Little T flew past me. Instinct had me drop the bag and run after Little T. Boy, was he fast! I didn't know what had just happened or where I was going, but I was on his heels because I was pretty fast myself.

By the time we stopped running, we were walking down Flatbush Avenue really fast. T put some money in my hand and said, "Put it in your pocket, and don't let niggas know you have it."

Two minutes later, Screw, BB, and Little ran up to us. "Yo, what's good?" asked BB. "What you catch, T?"

"About two hundred, I think. I didn't really count it yet," T said.

"We've got this purse, and I hope it's loaded. Damn, near had to knock the white bitch's teeth out to get it," BB shot back.

"I caught a wallet," Little joined in.

Screw said, "Yo, bend this corner here so we can see what's up."

Between the $150 Little T claimed, the $300 Little had caught, and the $800 that was in the purse, niggas were happier than a motherfucker. Half of the take would go to the ones who had put in the work. Well, at least that was the way it was *supposed* to go. Didn't always work out that way for everybody.

Little T had put in his work, so he automatically got $75. BB and Screw had caught the purse, so they got $200 each. Little was supposed to automatically get $150, but BB took control over Little's catch and added it to the pot. That's the type of shit that went down when we didn't man up when we needed to. So that left $775 to be split five ways, though no one said it would be split equally. BB, Screw, and Little T got $200 each. They gave Little $100, which made him angry—but he didn't say anything, which is the reason he was being herbed in the first place.

Screw handed me $75 and said in his Sho'nuff voice, "Bring nothing to the table, you get nothing to eat. It's only 'cause it's your first time out that I'm looking out for you. And besides, I fuck with you, Leroy."

"Next time make sure you put in work, and then your cut will be more—or you won't get a cut at all," BB told me.

Shit, little did he know that I was happier than a pig in shit with the $75 split, along with the money that Little T had already given me. That was more money than I'd ever had in my entire life. If nothing else, I could go and buy me a new book bag and jacket, and my mom's would be none the wiser. This was turning out to be a great experience. Well, at least I thought it was, but the day wasn't over yet.

G-baby woke up thinking it had all been a dream. But when he heard his mother crying through the door, he knew that it had really happened. He knocked on her bedroom door and called out, "Ma?"

"Hold on, Gerald. I'm coming," she said.

"I'm just making sure you're okay." He headed downstairs, as hungry as hell. G-baby knew that he would need to smoke a blunt and a half that night to help fight back the tears. As he walked into the kitchen, he could hear his mom's coming down the stairs.

"What are you looking for?" she asked.

"I'm hungry." His head was buried in the refrigerator.

"Go on and get out of the way," she said. "I'll fix something and call you when I'm done."

Back in his room, G-baby's mind was on the bag that had been under his bed since his uncle had dropped it off. Curiosity was killing him, but he had never looked in the bag. In fact, he had never looked in *any* of the bags that his uncle had dropped off from time to time. He'd always just put them under his bed and waited for his uncle to come back and pick them up. But that would never happen again, and that thought made tears run down G-baby's face as he reached under the bed and pulled the bag out.

It would be an understatement to say that G-baby was *surprised* at what he found upon opening the bag—four blocks of a white substance that he believed to be cocaine. But there was also something else underneath his bed. He sat there in amazement, mind racing, not knowing what to do next. His mother's fourth yell him brought him back to reality, and he went downstairs to eat.

Spider sat in that chair for hours before deciding it was time to make a move. He finally thought about Vito and figured he needed to give him a call. "Yo V, my man," he said when Vito picked up the phone.

Vito had just put a pie in the oven for the customer in front of him. "Hey, Spider, what's happening?"

"Man, I need to talk to you. I've got bad news," said Spider. "What's wrong?"

"They've killed Hulk."

There was a long pause, and finally Vito said, "Meet me at the house by ten thirty."

Spider said, "You bet." Then he hung up the phone and headed to their stash house. When he walked through the door, the aroma of marijuana was overwhelming, and he made a mental note to do something about that. His concern was about the nose candy. He knew that thirty bricks had just been dropped off, but he didn't know if Hulk had touched them yet. Hulk had been one hell of a businessman.

He made sure to get Vito out of the way and another delivery was being made before they could finish what they already had. He looked under the floor where the fresh drop was, and it hadn't been touched. Then he went to the other spot in the floor, and there were still fifteen bricks in there. When he checked the safe in the wall, Spider was amazed at the amount of money that was in there. He didn't know if Hulk had kept his own money in there with the re-up money, so he began to count.

After two and a half hours of counting, Spider was sure that the amount on the paper matched the amount in the bundle. There was $340,000 in the safe. Then he reached for the book in which Hulk had recorded how much drugs they had and how much money needed to get back to Vito. The book indicated that $200,000 was for the heroin, which they were out of; $75,000 was for the marijuana; and the remaining $65,000 was Spider's cut. Instead of recording names in the book, Hulk had used *you* to refer to Spider and *me* for himself.

Just looking at his brother's handwriting caused Spider to feel emotional about the sudden events. It was getting late—9:45, to be exact. He thought that he'd better be on his way to Vito and that he'd take the money with him.

On the way to Vito's spot, all Spider could think about was his brother, a real nigga and good friend. He was going to miss Hulk tremendously. He was also going to make sure that whoever was responsible for his brother's death paid dearly. In the end, they would *beg* for Spider to kill them.

Upon reaching Vito's spot, Spider gathered himself and walked up the driveway. Still in a daze, he didn't even notice Franky coming from behind the tree. That made him uncomfortable, because he didn't like anyone being able to sneak up on him. Franky extended his hand as he expressed his condolences for Spider's loss. When Spider got to the door, he didn't have to knock. Paully opened the door for him and did the same as Franky. Spider just wanted to get this over with so he could find Spaz and see what the word on the street was.

When Spider entered the living room, Vito was sitting in front of a bottle with two spliffs in the ashtray. Vito was as cool as hell for an Italian.

At that moment, Spider thought about when they all had first met. He and Hulk had been chillin' on the block when Vito's car had come speeding around the corner, caught a flat, and slammed into the parked cars. Spider had heard the sirens getting closer. Springing into action, Hulk had run across the street, pulled Vito out of the car, and told him, "Come with me." Spider hadn't known what Hulk was up to, but he had grabbed the door to the building so his brother and Vito could enter. Vito had been too shaken up to resist; otherwise he probably would've preferred to take his chances running from the police, rather than following Hulk's big black ass into a building in the hood.

As the door had closed behind Hulk and Vito, police were coming from everywhere. They'd even had the nerve to ask if Spider had seen where the white guy had gone, but Spider had ignored them as if they were speaking another language. When the police had retrieved two revolvers off the passenger seat of Vito's car, Spider had thought, *Damn, I should've grabbed them first!* Little did he know that Vito had just done a hit on two other Italians and that the police had chased him a long way from home.

Meanwhile, Hulk had taken the white dude up to his family's crib. Hulk and Spider's mother was in the kitchen and didn't know a white man was in the house until their pain-in-the-ass sister had screamed, "Who the hell is this white man? And what the hell is he doing here?"

Hulk had told her to be quiet, but the damage was done. Their mother had walked into Hulk and Spider's room and asked, "What the hell is going on here?"

Hulk could have told her anything and she'd have believed him. "Some dudes were chasing him and trying to rob him, so I brought him here to save him," he had said.

"So you bring him here? I hear the police outside. Why didn't you leave him to them?" "I thought he'd be better off with me," Hulk had replied.

Ma had been skeptical, but she had left it alone and said, "Boy, don't be bringing no bullshit to my house." Then she had headed back to the kitchen.

"Spider? Spider!" Vito had to call him twice to bring him out of his trance. Motioning for Spider to have a seat, Vito grabbed a spliff and slid the ashtray toward him. Spider handed the bag of money to Vito before he sat down.

Vito said, "Later. Tell me what happened to your brother."

While smoking the spliff, Spider told Vito what he knew. When he finished, Vito yelled for Paully, whispered something in his ear, and then turned his attention back to Spider.

"I'll get my people on it and give you whatever information they turn up," Vito told Spider.

"But in the meantime, do you think you can handle the operation by yourself? We've known each other a long time now, and no offense, but Hulk is the one who kept things in order. You guys have done a lot for me and made us a lot of money. When this is over, why don't you retire? Go open up a store or something. I can get your money cleaned up so the feds don't come kickin' down your door. What do you think?"

Spider said, "I appreciate that and I'll think about it."

"Don't think too hard—just do it. These streets are changing," said Vito. "Leave them to the younger ones. Haven't you done enough? Your brother is gone. Take what you've got and live, my friend."

"I'm living, Vito, and I'm not afraid of these streets. Plus we just got thirty in, and I've got to manage that."

"What? Here in the bag?" Vito asked.

"No, that's two hundred large for the heroin."

"You guys have brought me a lot of money, and you've played a part in me becoming who I am today. I'd like to see you retire, at least. When you're done with that thirty, pay me for twenty-five, and then you go and live."

Spider said, "I'll think about it, Vito—and again, I appreciate it."

"Yo, we've been walking forever," I said as we came up on Empire Boulevard. "Word," Little replied.

At that moment, Screw noticed the bus coming. "Our chariot awaits," he said, and we dashed across the street and waited by the bus stop. When we climbed on the back of the bus, however, we had no idea who was already on it. We were just tired and thankful that a bus had come along, but we were not thankful for what was about to go down.

All five of us had gotten on the bus before Screw and BB realized that the back of the bus was filled with them Parkside niggas. The only one I recognized was Johnny from my science class, but he wasn't looking friendly at all. You could cut the air with a knife, the tension was so thick. Everybody had gotten quiet, but that silence was quickly broken with a "What's up now?"

It was on, and we were trapped. All we could do was fight—and fight we did, as the bus made its way down Flatbush Avenue. People on the street could see niggas going at it as the bus drove by. In that tight space, it was crazy. I was catching blows from every direction, but giving them back just the same. It got so crazy that the driver finally stopped the bus in the middle of the street and got off without unlocking the back door. We were fighting for our lives at that point, struggling to get to the front door as innocent people were trying to get off the bus as well.

Then the rumble spilled off the bus and onto the street. Just as I got off, someone yelled "Knife!" Everybody had made it off the bus, or so I thought, giving us room and opportunity to pick up anything lying around to defend ourselves. When a dude knocked me to the ground right next to a car, I saw a pipe sticking out from under the vehicle. Before the dude could put the stomp on me, I swung that pipe and hit him on the knee, which gave me the couple of seconds I needed to get back to my feet. I was swinging that pipe like a madman, inching my way down Flatbush Avenue.

I looked to my left and saw that two dudes had Screw pinned up against a store, and they were giving him the business. Little T was a little farther up, working this dude till he hit the ground. "Roll out," I heard. I smacked the dude in front of me across the face with the pipe, turned, and kicked one of the dudes who had Screw pinned. The other dude caught a pipe to the back of the head. Then I tagged Screw's arm and said, "Let's go."

Little T was ahead of us, hauling ass down Flatbush. I don't know where I found the energy, but I was trying my best to catch up to him, with Screw by my side every step of the way. As we crossed Church Avenue, I was beginning to feel like I couldn't run anymore. Screw must've felt it too, but he said, "Just keep running, little nigga."

We were passing Erasmus Hall High School and a bunch of dudes. Little T was moving so fast that he didn't realize that he had just run past his two brothers. They got his back as Big T blunted, but then realized his little brother was in trouble. As we went by, Screw half yelled, "They after us." Big T looked up the block and saw the swarm chasing us, and he and his brother's boys put an end to the chase immediately.

Finally we were so out of breath that we truly couldn't run anymore. My heart was beating so hard that I felt like I was going to die. "Shit, where's BB and Little?" I asked Screw between heaves.

"I don't know," he said. "Come on, we're not out of the woods yet."

I didn't like the sound of that, but I definitely couldn't run anymore. I could barely catch my breath and walk, let alone fight or run. If I had never prayed before, I sure was praying at that moment to make it home.

When we finally reached Cortelyou Road train station, there was yet another large crowd. Little T was standing in the middle, telling the crew what had just gone down. Screw proceeded to cross the street to join them.

"I'm going home," I said.

"All right. A lot for your first day, huh?" Screw said with a chuckle.

As I walked along, I was thinking, *Shit, "first day"? This may be my last.* My body had already began to hurt, but as I saw my reflection in the grocery store window, I knew that I probably had one more fight ahead of me. This one I would definitely lose.

Little T was still telling the crew about what had happened when Screw rolled up. Everybody was there including Spank, Boy Boy, and Trouble—the ones who had gotten separated earlier in the day.

"We could've used some help from you guys with them faggot-ass Parkside niggas," Screw said. Then he noticed one nigga who didn't have a scratch on him, who was just chillin' like it was all good. Enraged, Screw asked, "Yo, Little, what's good? What happened to you? And where's BB?"

Little began to get nervous. He had dipped off the bus right behind the bus driver and made his way back without a scratch. Furthermore, he had no clue what had happened to BB. "I, I was going—"

A blow to the mouth from Little T shut him up. Screw then kicked him in the nuts, and Little T and Screw began to beat the shit out of him while everyone else watched and commented. "Bitch-ass nigga … Told you he wasn't down … Kick his fucking ass …" When they were finished, Screw went into Little's pockets and took back the money they had caught earlier. When he counted it to split with Little T, Screw realized that Little had $200 more than he should have. And with one last kick to the midsection, he said, "Don't come back around, Little. You're no longer welcome." They left Little lying there, beat up real bad, and headed down Cortelyou Road.

Coming toward them was Pop, the unofficial leader of the crew. Pop was that dude who had all the girls. He could fight better than most of the crew—and anyone who was better didn't dare let it show. Pop would never let it die. He had a heart beyond heart, and family was everything to him. He was also extremely charismatic, so everybody liked Pop. He never abused his authority, and even when he could make something happen to you, he didn't always make the call. When he *did* make a call, niggas listened. Pop was well respected in the hood.

"Look at these wild guys coming down the street," Pop said as they all gave him a dap. As they were chillin' in front of the pizza spot and giving Pop the rundown, Tracey came up and said that she had seen BB being put into an ambulance on the avenue.

She was so dramatic. "There was blood everywhere. I heard the police say that it looked like a horror movie on the bus. Some other dude was being put into an ambulance too, but I don't think he made it." Tracey was a bad bitch, and everybody usually had something slick to say to her. But the news she had just dropped on the crew made niggas angry, so nobody was thinking about her ass at that moment. Besides, she had eyes only for Pop, like most of the chicks who were down.

As Tracey was leaving and everybody was caught up in their thoughts about BB, Shontay came up the block. She was angry as hell 'cause none of the crew had showed up for her party. "What the fuck happened to you guys? I had a crib full of horny bitches with no dicks in sight," she complained, but no one paid her much attention.

"Not now, Tay," Pop said. When Shontay tried to continue, he said "Not now!" in a stern voice. She shut up and stormed away mad.

It took two days for my mom's to notice my busted lip and the fact that I wasn't wearing my new jacket. "Boy, what happened to your face? I know you're not out there fighting," she said, as a smack caught me in that same busted lip, reopening it and causing it to bleed. She landed a few more blows before she realized that, first, I didn't have on the new jacket she had bought, and second, the book bag I had didn't look like the one she had bought either.

I took a major ass whipping to start my day off, which sent me out into the world a very angry kid. I thought, *Damn, she beat my ass when she should've been concerned with why I had a busted lip. She don't give a fuck 'bout me. All she does is kick my ass. I get my ass kicked more at home than I ever did in the street. At least they had reason for beating a nigga's ass. What was hers?*

When I got outside, G-baby was already there waiting so we could walk to school together.

"Damn, son, what happened to you?" "My mom's. Come on," I replied.

G-baby thought, *Damn, she beats his ass worse than niggas. No wonder he goes so hard on a nigga. He's tired of getting his ass whipped.*

We headed to school in silence. G-baby didn't know what to say to make me feel better, and I was too hot because of another unjustified ass whipping. I felt a tap on my shoulder, and G-baby was passing me a blunt. "Don't get blood on that shit," he said. As much as I wanted to laugh, I just couldn't.

When we reached Coney Island Avenue, a lot more dudes than usual were there. Even Pop was there, but I hadn't been introduced to him yet. I shared a couple of classes with his little brother, but I didn't know that yet either.

Screw came up to us and said, "Sorry for your loss, G-baby. Yo, Leroy was trying to imitate Sho'nuff, but he wasn't as good as BB. You know, BB's in the hospital hurt up pretty bad. We're gonna set it on them niggas today. Are you down?"

I looked at G-baby, who must've understood that that was more of a demand than a request, no matter how cool Screw had been when he asked.

"Later," G-baby said. Then he proceeded to school, as high as hell and thinking to himself, *I hope he makes it.*

Spraga was an impatient man with little tolerance for incompetence. He was pacing his office and pulling on a big head, but no amount of marijuana could relieve the anxiety he felt as he awaited his gunmen's return. He had sent them on a job for payback for his missing eye and his wife being killed a few years earlier.

Intruders had entered his house and pistol-whipped him so bad that he had lost an eye, but that wasn't what had made him give up the location of the stash. It was when they had shot his beloved wife that he had known those niggas meant business. He had been a small-timer with connections out the ass on the come up. In America for only three years, he already had four kilos and 203 pounds of marijuana in stash. There had been ninety grand in one of the pillows he slept on, but they had missed that.

"Take it," he had said, "just take it," as he had crawled over to his wife's limp body. At that point, he couldn't have cared less about the drugs. His wife had been priceless in his eyes and heart. He had thought, *If these pussy holes let me live, me gone kill dem, their children, and their children's children.*

Hulk and Spider had come up like Vito had said they would. It took years for Spraga to pinpoint exactly who was responsible, but he was the main distributor of marijuana across BK when Hulk and Spider had begun to do their numbers, and all fingers pointed to them. Spraga thought, *If it wasn't them, oh well. Me gone too long without payback. Jus' be two dead pussy holes.*

A knock at his door brought him out of his trance. When only two gunmen entered, he knew something had gone wrong, and he became enraged. He met them in the center of his office, and the look on his face said, "This better be good."

"Boss, me not know wha happen. They went in and only two came out. Den dis big pussy hole start licking shot pon de car. Dras was hit, so me knew me had to done him suppose. Trigga shot him like you say. But we couldn't even make it in before a whole heap of blood eat gunshot start. Dras push me, and like him say, some big blood clot man chase me down, licking shot like mad."

Stiggy's recounting of the story only added fuel to Spraga's fire. *Pow!* One shot to Stiggy's head made sure there would be no more fuckups from him.

Then Spraga got in Driver's face and said, "De nex time me send you out, you betta come back wit propa results. Be gone."

Disappointed, Spraga sat and waited in his chair as his men removed the dead body. Then he picked up the phone and told Gully that he needed him.

"Yo, Pop, this is the little nigga I was telling you about." Screw was introducing me to Pop when he spotted the crowd of dudes coming toward us. There were like fifteen to twenty of them chanting, "What's the flava? Decep."

Pop stepped up and said, "Hi, cousin," and gave me a dap. Pop had placed a call to his aunt's house in Fort Greene and notified his cousin that he needed his help with a situation. He knew that his cousin was a menace who ran with some menacing dudes. Seemed like a couple of dudes put in calls to their people. We had niggas from Vanderveer, Fort Greene, Washington Avenue, Troop Avenue—seemed like everywhere.

I was thinking, *What the fuck did Screw need me for?* There were like seventy dudes on that corner, so many that the police were driving by slow and watching niggas.

Pop was like, "Let's move before the wagons come." The shit was crazy. There were so many niggas going down Coney Island Avenue, making noises, introducing one another, and talking about what they were going to do to them niggas. You would've thought that school had let out.

Pop had also talked Shontay into having her girlfriends back over, so that they could entertain until we were due to go and set it on them niggas. When we reached Shontay's crib, she was stunned and immediately objected to the number of niggas Pop had with him. "Where the fuck do you think all these niggas are going, Pop?"

Pop put his arm around her and kicked it in her ear for a minute. She smiled and then just said, "They'd better not fuck up my parents' house, Pop."

"I got you," he said, knowing good and well that her crib was probably going to get fucked up and looted before all the niggas left. Things were cool at first, but with the consumption of alcohol and marijuana and it getting closer to game time, niggas got more rowdy. There were only like fifteen women to accommodate all them niggas, and you could hear screams over the music playing.

I was in the corner of the couch, not drinking or smoking too much, and hoping that I wouldn't have to use the bathroom. Obtaining a seat happened only when somebody got up. You could see niggas who'd been standing for a while scramble for a spot as soon as a person rose. It was so funny to me, like niggas were playing musical chairs and shit. Every so often, Little T or Screw would pass me a blunt or 40, disappear, and then come back for it. They were having a ball.

Then Pop spotted me, and I guess he needed or wanted to kick it with me. "Yo, let me get right here," he said to a dude, and the dude got up.

I thought, *Damn, this nigga gets much respect.* Then Pop asked, "What's up, little nigga?"

I gave him the head nod.

"I've heard some good shit about you. Do you go to Ditmas?"

"Yeah," I said, "my little brother goes there."

"Listen, when we get out there, stay close and alert," Pop said. "Do what you've been doing, represent, and don't get scared."

I thought, *Easy for you to say.*

Pop said, "Shit's going to be simple, 'cause they ain't expecting this shit. We gonna smash them bitch-ass niggas and get out of there. I hear you're pretty fast too." Before I could respond, Shontay was pulling him away, leading him upstairs through the crowd of people.

No sooner had Pop risen than two niggas tried to get his seat, and one of them would've ended up on my lap if I hadn't pushed his ass away. "My bad," the nigga said, and went and posted up waiting for someone else to rise.

The next few hours seemed to fly by, and it seemed like Pop was upstairs with Shontay the whole time. Finally he came down the stairs, repeating over and over, "It's about that time." Niggas was ready.

As we all left Shontay's crib, Pop observed that a few niggas were leaving with more than they had arrived with, although Shontay seemed oblivious to that. When her parents came home later and noticed most of their valuables were missing, she'd have some explaining or serious lying to do. But at the moment Shontay was happy because niggas hadn't fucked up her crib, except for the fridge.

Shontay didn't live far from the corner of Parkside and Ocean Avenue, where those other niggas had gathered to kick it. School had let out, so the crowd coming toward those niggas didn't set off an alarm until it was too late. Thirty or more of them were on the corner as we approached, and the Fort Greene niggas were up front so those other niggas didn't recognize the danger coming their way.

In an instant, it was on. One of the Fort Greene niggas let a mini hammer slide out of his sleeve into his hand. He asked, "What's up, bitch?" as he smashed into a dude's face, ending that dude's fight immediately. Some fought and others tried to run, but there was no escaping. There were just too many of us. At first I was lost, because there wasn't anybody for me to hit. But a few more in front of the train station tried to come to their boys' rescue, only to receive the worst beat-downs of their lives.

I was standing in a doorway, and as one came running up, I stepped out and caught him in the face. Between his momentum and the power of my blow, he was lifted clean off his feet—and I had released my anger from the ass whipping I was taking at home.

It was crazy out there. Dudes were getting stabbed and hit with mini hammers and bats, bottles were being broken over niggas' heads, and milk crates were being swung and thrown. Dudes were being hit by cars as they tried to get away from the craziness. The battle continued until the sirens from the wagons could be heard, and even that didn't stop some niggas.

I found myself racing down Ocean Avenue with a bunch of dudes, trying to escape the police. Behind me, dudes were laid out in the streets everywhere, and leading the escaping pack was— Who else?—Little T's fast ass. A police car had jumped the curb trying to cut him off, but Little T jumped and slid across the hood. When his feet hit the sidewalk, they must've been moving too fast for him, because he stumbled and fell. The cops exited their vehicles, and one tried to grab anyone he could as we flew past him. The other cop grabbed Little T, but someone hit the cop in the back of the head as they went by, so Little T was off and running again.

That nigga was so fast that he passed me. I couldn't keep up with him, but I followed him from a distance. He turned off Ocean Avenue, so when I got to the corner, I tuned off Ocean Avenue. He dipped down East Eighteenth, so I dipped down East Eighteenth. He dipped into a house's backyard and I followed. *Man!* Was I grateful that he stopped running, 'cause I was tired and feeling the pain in my lungs. When he saw that it was me following him, he tried to laugh, but he was out of breath and could only smile. We stayed in that backyard for a while, first to catch our breath and let our heart rates get back to normal, and second to allow the police to do what they had to do.

With all of the activity, I had almost forgot that my mom's was off work that day. My school wasn't but five minutes from our crib, and it was four thirty in the afternoon. Again, I knew that my battles were far from over.

When I walked through the door at home, I was met with a blow to my face. "Where the hell have you been? And don't lie saying school, because I walked up there and you were nowhere to be found." Another blow. "And what's this I hear about you beating up on people? I don't send you out of this house to be a bully. You fucking know better." A few more blows. "I hope your ass had fun, 'cause you got yourself on punishment. Go to your room, and don't turn on that goddamn TV either."

I was beginning to hate that woman, which was creating an inner struggle for me. She didn't realize that she was creating the menace that I was becoming.

"Yo, Vito, let me use your phone," said Spider.

Deuce's sister was asleep on the couch when the phone rang, but the noise shook her awake. "Hello?"

"Hey, baby girl," said Spider.

"Hey, Daddy." She was happy to hear his voice, especially since she rarely got a chance to see him.

Spider asked, "Where's Trey?"

"I don't know. Hold on." She ran down the hallway to Deuce's room, but he wasn't there. Then she opened the door leading to the upstairs apartments and yelled "Deuce!" a couple of times. Finally she heard a faint "Yeah." Deuce and his boys had passed out, and her yelling woke everybody up. She heard him coming and ran to the phone. "He's coming, Daddy. So when will I see you?"

"Soon, baby girl," replied Spider. "Real soon."

Hearing Deuce enter the apartment, she yelled, "Dad's on the phone."

"Why do you have to be loud?" asked Deuce, going into his room and picking up the phone. His sister sounded like such a little girl when she was talking to their father, even though she was sixteen. "Hello?"

"What's up, Trey?" asked Spider. "Same ol', Pops."

"Listen, I know that your uncle dropped off some money for you. Take it and open a bank account for your sister."

Little did Spider know that Deuce's mother had already done that before she died, and that Deuce had always put a couple of grand in it when his uncle came to re-up him, as Hulk had insisted that he do. It was crazy, like his uncle was his pops and his pops was his uncle. Deuce had little respect for his father, but he'd always had the utmost respect for his uncle Hulk. "Aight, Pops," he said.

"Give me a few days," said Spider. "I've got a lot of shit to handle, but then I'll be by there to see you and baby girl."

"Aight, Pops."

"Hey Trey, I'm thinking about moving y'all out of there and selling that place. Shit is getting crazy, and I can't afford to lose you or baby girl."

"Aight, Pops," and Deuce hung up the phone. Then he sat on the edge of the bed thinking, *He's got another thing coming if he thinks he's selling this crib. I'm cool with him getting baby girl out of here, but I'm not fucking going anywhere. This is my mom's crib, which makes it my crib now. This is where I get it in, where I feel safe. Man, fuck that shit.*

When Spider hung up, he was thinking, *Damn, I've got to do better by them. And I believe it's time they met their little twin brothers and sisters who live in Bed-Stuy.* They weren't exactly little—the twin boys were about to turn seventeen, and their sisters had just turned fifteen.

"Everything okay?" Vito asked, bringing Spider out of his thoughts. "Yeah, just touching base with my kids."

The mention of kids made Vito think about Hulk's crazy-ass son Killa. "Hey, ain't your nephew coming home soon?" he asked, already knowing the answer.

Vito was in the Mob and made it his business to know everybody else's business, so that gave him connections everywhere. He had already put out the word to the right people to take care of inmate 12B4367. Not that Killa needed it, but when you were up north, anything could happen. To have the police looking out for you was better than any banger you could create to protect yourself.

Spider said, "Yeah—Thursday, to be exact."

"You need to try to control him," advised Vito. "I'm sure he's not taking his father's death lightly, and he's going to want revenge."

Spider said, "He doesn't know yet." At least, that's what he assumed. On the other hand, he knew that niggas in the pen knew everything going on in the streets. Shit, most of the time they knew *more* than the niggas on the street.

"Not smart, Spider," said Vito. "How can you keep that information from him?" Everybody knew a man like Hulk, even people who had never met him. "Whether or not you truly understand it, you and your brother were in the big leagues—and you still are. You've got to think bigger and smarter, Spider. You have to be two steps ahead of them streets."

The convo began to piss off Spider, who didn't need a lecture right then. "Well, if he was so fucking smart, how did he get killed? And if you're so fucking smart, who did it?" With that, he stormed out the door.

Vito didn't have answers to Spider's questions, but he intended to find out. And as soon as Spider paid for their last shipment, their business was over.

When Batman woke, he decided to go tell his mom's about Hulk being killed. He knew she wouldn't take it well, but he figured it was best to just go ahead and get it over with. When he entered his mom's crib, everything was turned off except the living room TV.

Batman's mom's was staring at the TV with tears in her eyes, rocking back and forth. She knew that her son was there, but she never looked at him.

"Are you okay, Ma?" Batman asked. "He's dead, isn't he?"

"Yeah, Ma."

She began crying. She had a heavy load on her chest that she had hoped Hulk would address one day, but now he'd never get the chance.

She gathered herself and prepared to drop a bomb. "Sit down, son. I need to talk to you." Batman sat down next to his mommas, who continued to rock back and forth.

Then, in a low, shaky voice, she began: "Twenty-one years ago, before you were born, I made one of the biggest mistakes of my life."

The start of the story made Batman feel uneasy, and his mom's paused before continuing. "I was dating this guy who I knew was no good, but I fell in love with him anyway. I was only seventeen and dumb as hell. He had other women and a baby mama, but his mac was tight and he insisted that he was dealing with his baby mama like that. One day I was coming up the block when I saw him coming out of the store, all hugged up and having a grand ol' time with his baby mama."

She really began to cry at that moment and paused again before she continued. "I began to cry as I followed him, trying to decide if I wanted to run up on his ass. When I reached the corner and was about to cross the street, someone came up from behind and grabbed my arm. It was my guy's brother, and out of anger I said to myself, *I'll fix his ass*. Crying the entire time, I let him lead me away in the opposite direction. He ended up walking me back home, and we stood in front of my building for a while with him holding me and saying it would be all right. Finally I grabbed his hand, led him inside, and let him make love to me."

Batman wasn't stupid, but his heart wouldn't let his mind piece together what she was trying to tell him.

His mom's continued, "That was the first and last time we ever did it. When we finished, I felt so ashamed of myself. I had just slept with my guy's brother, for God's sake. Your grandmother kept yelling at me, 'You'd better get a father in here to take care of that baby. I'm struggling to feed the mouths I already have.' Your grandfather wanted to know who it was so he could make him take the responsibility like a man. They were so disappointed in me. I avoided both guys until I was five months pregnant. They were always together, and I just knew that my guy's brother had told him that he'd slept with me—and that they both looked at me as a big ol' whore. When I finally got up the nerve to confront the situation, I really didn't know what to do. I had no way of knowing which of them was responsible for you—and still don't, to this day."

Batman was getting angry and wished she'd just spit it out. If she had ever looked at him, she might not have continued.

She said, "So I went to the corner where they hung out—"

Unable to take any more of the storytelling, Batman's anger overcame him. "Just spit it out.

Who are they?"

Between sober and heavy tears, she said the words he didn't want to hear: "Hulk and Spider."

Angry as hell, Batman wanted to get up, but he was crippled by what his mother had just unloaded on him. His mind was racing, but one thought kept coming back. *My best friend could be my brother or cousin.*

Since Batman hadn't stormed away, she continued her story. "When I confronted them about the situation, Hulk snapped and began to beat the shit out of Spider. He kept saying, 'Why the fuck didn't you tell me that you fucked her?' When their boys finally got Hulk off Spider, the rage in his eyes sent me running home crying. Neither of them spoke to me for years, though Spider would drop off a few dollars when he could. I guess he felt that no matter what, he was still family—and he knew that Hulk wasn't going to do it. We weren't doing anything, but Hulk would always catch Spider coming from my building, and they would get into a fight. I guess the ass whippings finally got the best of Spider, because eventually he stopped coming by. About that same time, Deuce's mother had moved up the block. Hulk went by your grandparents' house and gave me some keys and an address on a piece of paper."

Batman wasn't really listening. He was still trying to absorb the fact that either Hulk or Spider was his father and that he'd probably never know which one. He finally found the strength to rise.

She thought he was leaving, so she yelled, "Your little brother is definitely Hulk's son."

He had already figured that out, since he had seen the creeping between Hulk and his mother before his brother was born. Instead of going to his apartment, Batman went to his old bedroom.

There was a knock at the door. "Come," Spraga said.

Gully entered and said, "Wha gwan, boss man? Ya call fa me?"

Gully knew how to follow instructions and get things done, and Spraga knew it. He had sent Gully out before, and although the man hadn't been able to get Spider, he had gotten Spider's bitch. That had provided Spraga with a little satisfaction, but now he wanted revenge. He wanted Spider, Spider's sons, and Hulk's sons dead, and he wanted the girls kidnapped and raped. Until then, he wouldn't be completely satisfied.

Spraga told Gully, "We have unfinished business wit den pussyhole boys dem. Me specially want dat boy Killa, end dat blood clot bloodline." He had tried to have Killa killed while he was in prison, but it hadn't worked. "You can handle dis."

"You done know," Gully replied.

Killa was in his cell, burning up inside. Just as they had begun to connect on a deeper level, his father was gone. It was killing him inside. The thought of the mighty Hulk being dead was unimaginable. Killa could see someone wanting to do something to him or his cousin Deuce, or even his older cousins Spaz or Dropout. But Pops? That was a lot for him to swallow, and he couldn't wait for the next three and a rise to come.

Killa remembered his father talking to him, trying to prepare him for life and what it really meant to be a man. For the first time, Hulk had thought that he was getting through to his son. He had shared with Killa the fact that there had been some things kept from him—in fact, kept from everybody. Hulk had some keys, numbers, and bank accounts that Killa needed to see, just in case something happened to Hulk.

Damn, I never thought I'd be needing that shit so soon, thought Killa.

Most of the fellas made it back to Coney Island Avenue with a few scrapes and bruises. A few got caught and arrested, but ultimately the rumble went well for them. Pop sent one dude on a mission to the weed spot on Newark and Argyle Avenue, and another dude was sent to the store for 40s and blunts. Then niggas sat out there getting fucked up for hours, celebrating what they felt was a victory.

Meanwhile the few Parkside dudes who weren't seriously injured or locked up were having their own gathering, one of defeat and anger. They all threw in their two cents about how to get them niggas back. But underneath the anger and adrenaline, none of them wanted any more of what they had gone through that day.

The next morning I awoke feeling like I had been in a fight, but not with the Parkside dudes.

My mom's was still on her shit. "You think your ass is smart? You think I'm raising some type of hoodlum in my house? You've got another thing coming, mister. From now on, you'll be going to your grandmother's house after school. In fact, you're going over there straight after school today, so your ass better come straight home."

Just like clockwork, G-baby was at the window calling for me. I finished getting myself together and headed out the door. When he saw me, all he said was, "Daaaaaamn, all that happened yesterday?"

"Yeah, but them dudes didn't do it," I replied.

G-baby probably thought, *Damn, his mom's be fucking him up worse than a nigga could.* I'm sure he felt for me, his homeboy. But there was nothing he could do about it, so he just passed me a blunt as we walked to school.

When we reached the corner of Coney Island Avenue, Screw and Pop were there chilling with a couple other regular dudes. When they saw me, they assumed that my black eye came from the rumble.

Pop said, "Damn, Little L, you got in it yesterday, huh?" Without waiting for a response, he put an arm around me and walked with us to the school. "Yo, I'm feelin' your heart, L. If anybody—I mean *anybody*—fucks wit you, you let us know. You're one of us now, and we take care of ours." He gave me a dap of confirmation, then continued, "BB made it home last night, but he's still fucked up pretty bad. We're going over there to holla at him. I'll be sure to tell him how you represented for him."

"Cool," I said. Then me and G- baby proceeded to school, with me filling him in on Mom's latest strike of genius.

He was like, "Damn! Well, at least she isn't going to change your school. We can still hang for a minute before you have to bounce."

"Yeah, I guess," I replied.

I spent the whole day thinking about being at my grandmother's house. She was cool, I ate well, we did stuff together, and she didn't give me any ass whippings, but she was tight as hell with me going outside. I could see the other kids on the block playing and having fun, but my boundary was the front of the house. A few dudes came and introduced themselves—Tallman, Chipmunk, Ant, C, and Drew. But past convo for a few minutes, I'd be left there alone to watch dudes have fun from a distance. That weekend was boring, and I could hardly wait for Monday so I could be with my friends.

As the sound of the gates was heard for the last time, freedom smelled like good pussy the morning after a murder. Killa stretched and spotted the Lincoln, and since he didn't see anything else, he figured that was his ride. As he walked toward the car, he thought about what he needed to do first.

When Killa got closer to the car, a gentleman jumped out, obviously prepared to follow his instructions. "Hello, sir," the man said as he opened the car door.

Climbing into the car, Killa noticed the absence of extravagance or lavish enticements. It was just a Lincoln—which wasn't fucked up, but he had figured for a bit more since he was just coming home. But by the time he reached his destination, he'd understand that what he had inherited couldn't be conveyed in a pickup from prison. In fact, he couldn't possibly have imagined …

As the driver got into his seat, he said, "Welcome, sir. It is my pleasure to be your driver today. I'd like you to sit back and enjoy your travels." A divider was going up between them, and a green screen was coming down.

Killa was in awe, seeing his father's face appear on the screen. Hulk seemed to look right at his son, as though they were sitting there in the limo together. As he began to speak, the car started moving. That ride enlightened Killa about the world into which he was being released. He was given a rundown on all the resources, finances, assets, and other details about his father's business, as well as what Hulk wanted his son to do at this point.

"What's up, son? I know that you're probably tripping right now in your head. You're seeing this only because something has happened to me, and there ain't no coming back. I love you, son, and you mean the world to me. You were my anchor in this shit. I knew, or at least hoped, that when my time came, you'd be ready to out-think the bitch ass, outclass with style and finesse, with a left to make any boxer impressed, with a gun that forever barks, bitch nigga get no reject." Hulk laughed and then said, "Pardon me, son. I got caught up in the moment, and it felt like dropping it on ya for a sec. But seriously speaking, I've got to further enlighten you about some important issues." As the laugh died, so did his attention to the present.

Swoooo went the sound of Gully inhaling the spliff. "Dem pussy hole reach yet?" he asked, growing impatient as he sat a block away and awaited the arrival of the family car. One too many spliffs and a one-on-one of that cain could prove to be the reason for his first major fuckup, which the boss wouldn't like.

The limo pulled up, and all that could be heard was the tires screeching out of the parking spot. They didn't give the chauffeur time to get out of the car. Gunshots erupted, penetrating the Lincoln with swiss cheese precision. The two-hundred-round clips from the Caleco assault rifle were sure to stop anything breathing inside that limo, but Gully knew what this hit meant to the boss man. So being Gully, he had his fifty-cal dessert waiting for this moment. He was sure he was gonna take the heads off them niggas, causing a definite closed casket situation and making the boss happier than a kid getting a new bike on Christmas morning. But as Gully looked into the limo and saw the gruesome aftermath of two-hundred-round clips in such a concentrated area, he hurled for the second time in his life. "We done fucked up now," he said as he got back into the car and sped away.

Monday came and went pretty much uneventfully. But my bus ride showed promise for excitement, entertainment, maybe even some drama.

Upon getting on the bus, I noticed a few dudes acting like they had the biggest nuts in the world. One thing I learned early on the streets was that if you look for trouble, it will find you— but it'll also come back the next day to see if you've had enough. I was outnumbered too much to engage my rage, but something told me that in time I wouldn't have to engage shit. Shit was gonna come knocking at my door without an invitation. For the time being, I just laughed at the antics of those dudes and their ability to fuck with people. None of the other people on the bus did anything but watch, clutch their bags, and hope *they* didn't get fucked with.

As a couple of weeks went by, this gang of misfits ignored my existence while terrorizing everyone around me. But one particular morning, I guess, was my morning. The stars were in line for my first, though not last, encounter with this band of wannabe—or I should say up-and- coming—thugs. Little did they know that I was up and coming too. Besides, at that point fear no longer lived in me. An encounter with them would be just another notch in my tree called "Remember me, bitch."

For the most part I was a problem resolver, not a problem starter, but when it was time to get money, I'd set it in a minute. Fuck with someone that I fuck with, I'd set it. A few times something just made me want to get at a nigga because of the personal shit I was going through. Regardless of my motivation, I went at a nigga with "Remember me, bitch" in my head, like that motherfucker had already done something to me.

On this particular morning, slush and invisible ice patches were everywhere. The last passenger was just climbing aboard when I noticed some kid running to catch the bus, and I turned to let the driver know to wait for him. Suddenly the kid slipped and both feet went up in the air, and after I thought he had recovered—*Boom!*—the motherfucker slipped again. His legs flew out from under him and he hit the concrete flat on his back, just as the bus began to roll away from the bus stop.

I just started laughing, but I guess I was the only person on that damn bus who saw the shit and thought it was hilarious as a motherfucker. Because what stopped my laughter was the sound of someone asking me, "What the fuck is so funny?" I was always big for my age, and sometimes my voice and laughter came out a lot louder than I intended.

While I had been absorbed in what was going on outside, something had been happening inside the bus. My fit of laughter happened just as one dude was getting punked by his fellow crew member. Not realizing that I was laughing at the kid outside, niggas thought I was laughing at their homeboy who was getting played in front of everybody. So the bigger dog in the crew said, "Who the fuck is that, and what the fuck is so funny?"

Then the cat who was getting punked asked, "Yeah, what the fuck is so funny?" I didn't realize at first that it was two different niggas asking the same question, and by the time I did, it was on and poppin'.

"What the fuck is so funny?" That question startled me out of my thoughts. Suddenly I realized that some dude I didn't know was kinda half bent over and repeating those words into my ear in a tone that instinctively put me on alert. My ability to speedily transition from joy in one moment to rage in the next has proved valuable throughout my life—but that was its debut appearance, and what a debut it was. Someone was whispering into my ear using the most aggressive tone he could muster without actually screaming.

I spoke no words and gave no warning. As I turned to look him in the eyes, my right hand prepared to deliver a perfect overhand. I turned and stood at the same time, and he didn't know what hit him. It couldn't have landed any better, especially in a bus packed half full of people.

He might not have known what happened, but his friends sure did. I heard "Get 'im!" and they all rushed in to either push or punch me. To keep the innocent from getting hurt, I held them off until I felt the bus slowing down. When I heard the *Ding!* of the back door unlocking for exit, I gave everyone the hardest shove that I could gather and shot out that door. Then the engine roared and the bus began to move away before any of them made it off.

So I got away with that one, but then I had to get from Flatbush to school in thirty minutes or else that wouldn't be my only fight of the day. That thought contributed to my athletic training, because I sprinted most of the distance and then appreciated myself for getting to school not a second late and avoiding another ass whipping from demon mom.

I tried to tell G-baby about what had happened, but he was kinda distracted by the death of his uncle. Then I was on a time clock to get back to Scram Jones's crib, which was Grandma's house, and I wasn't taking the bus or even following that route. I wasn't afraid of the inevitable confrontation, but I had enough sense to know that I wasn't Superman and couldn't have beat the eight or more—God knows how many—niggas who might have been waiting on my black ass. So I walked on Thursday and Friday, which was a welcome ending to an eventful week.

As I was walking home on Friday afternoon, I was feeling like the bus shit was gonna be my only excitement for the week. But just as I stepped onto Nostrand, someone ran into me. I didn't know who it was at first, but it turned out to be Little T followed by a few other homeboys—and the law in the distance.

"Oh shit, L, what are you doing over here?" he asked. Before I could answer, he tugged at my arm to run with him, and without thinking, I did. When we stopped running, we were a couple of blocks from Veer and along the bus route I had been avoiding. As that reality hit me, I got a little nervous, but I felt better at the sight of a few more of the homeboys I knew coming up, though I also noticed a few who didn't like me too much.

Niggas asked me, "Where the hell did you come from? You weren't there when the shit jumped off."

Little T jumped in and said, "I bumped into the nigga and pulled him along."

As we were talking, I was paying attention to the eyes of one dude who was watching me intensely. Little T saw him, too, and he asked me if the dude had a problem with me. When I said, "Yeah," he turned back to the dude and asked, "What problem you got with our boy?"

That question got the entire crowd's attention. The dude began telling so many lies that I had to intervene and tell the actual facts of the situation Then Little T asked the nigga, "Straight up, I know my son has no problem giving you a fair one. Are you trying to go there?"

Before the dude could say a word, one of his homeboys said, "I got this. I'll beat this nigga's ass today."

The homeboy was more my size and a little older, but my boys already knew how I gave it up.

So Little T didn't even look at me before saying, "Let's take it to the park."

As we were cutting through the Page to get to the park, his few homeboys were talking shit in front of me and my few homeboys. The dude charged at me, trying to catch me off guard, but little did he know that I stay on point.

I was peeping the shit talk, quieting down and the dude had kinda fallen behind his boys, so as he came up, I sidestepped to the left and sent out my right hand. I caught him right on the nose, but if I'd swung harder, I could've knocked his ass out. Still, it did enough damage to set him up with a two piece from hell. As the blows landed, everybody on my side was yelling "Oooooo!" and giving this brother room to work. When he paused, I slid back in front of the dude and hit him with a straight right hand, connecting beautifully with that already bruised nose. Instead of just falling backward, he caught himself on the second step and made the ultimate mistake, bending over enough for me to catch him with an uppercut that almost took his head off.

Fight done, the nigga was leaking like someone had left the faucet half open. If he hadn't flown into his homeboy, he would've hit the ground and busted his head wide open—possibly giving me a fucking case. One of his homeboys tried to run up on me from behind, but my boy FA, who I hadn't figured to be my boy at the time, hit the dude so hard that it stopped his momentum and he crumbled right on the spot.

Before the shit really got crazy, everybody heard that dreaded *Woop! Woop!* from the wagon full of 5-0 and got on their horses. Luckily for me, most of the crowd was headed back toward Flatbush, and I was going in the opposite direction. I slowed down after about two blocks, because all the sirens were chasing the crowd. That altercation put me an hour and five minutes late, and I still had about ten blocks to go. I didn't want to attract attention by running, though, since police were coming from everywhere and headed in the direction that I had just came from. As long as I played it cool, I could make it home and prepare for my next battle—for reaching home so late. Sucks being me!

The knocking on the door could've been from the police, abruptly breaking Spraga's enjoyment from the head that pretty fat-ass Latiesha was giving him. "Ah, who dat banging pos me blood clot door?" he asked, watching Latiesha's sexy ass get up off her knees.

"Gully," he heard from outside the door.

As he buzzed the door open and let Gully in, that fat ass was just jiggling its way toward the door. Through Spraga's head raced the thought, *Ya done know me need to beat dat.*

The sight of Gully brought him out of his daydream of waxing the fat ass, sexy figure, and pretty face of the woman prancing her way out of sight. The look on Gully's face, even with shades on, couldn't hide the man's anticipation. "Wha gwan, Gully?" asked Spraga. "Why you look so?"

Figuring he was about to be killed for fucking up, Gully paused and removed his shades. "Boss man, me think me done fucked up big time."

The look on the boss man's face said, "You'd better continue before death becomes your destination."

"Yo, me went an sat by the funeral home, jus' to chill an wait for the pussy hole dem," said Gully. "All right, the limo pulls up, we mash pon the scene, let go a whole heap a blood clot shot pon de limo."

"Okay, so wha?" said Spraga.

Gully said, "The pussy hole dem weren't in the car." Spraga's look seemed to intensify as Gully continued. "Yo, it was a bunch of blood clot white people. All the men made me think that it was the Mob. Me could see their guns when me look inside." Gully was confused by the boss man's face, which seemed more confused than angry.

Before Gully could wonder further about his own fate, however, the boss man began to laugh loudly and joyously. Now Gully was really confused, as Spraga rose out of his seat and approached him with open arms, laughing at what Gully had thought was a major fuckup.

As he hugged Gully, Spraga said, "If you did what you did to who I think you did it to, Jah works an me gone give ya double."

Gully was relieved, but also curious about who was in that limo—and a very old memory came to his mind.

The day had finally come, and Spider felt like, *Fuck it, I'll to try to keep him cool. But shit, that nigga now has the resources, money, and power to do whatever he feels like regarding his future.* Spider would guide and help as much as allowed, but he wasn't gonna let his nephew stress him out. Besides, he knew that Vito would keep an eye on him.

After the ride home, Killa had a new perspective on life and how to handle things. *They wanted to deal with my father's child, and now they will*, he told himself. As the limo pulled up he couldn't see much of a welcome home, but that changed when he walked through the unlocked door. "Welcome home!" roared through the place, where every inch of space was filled with people and furniture. Killa was almost amazed at the capacity, when he spotted his right hand, his man 50 grand. Come to find out he was actually family. Everything else had to take a pause for his greeting to one of the most important people in his life, right under his mom's and grandparents.

Killa cared about very few people in this world. Some folks had gained his respect, but nobody could ever mean as much to him as his cousin Deuce. The sight of Deuce made him remember the past and appreciate the present at the same time. Their dap and embrace moved the whole room, because those who knew them understood what that reunion meant to the world.

As the night simmered down, Deuce and Killa slid off to kick it. They replayed their entire lives together, right up to the day Killa had gone in. There wasn't much they hadn't gone through together, kinda like Spider and Hulk, and they just clung to each other.

Finally the moment came, and Killa said, "Yo, cuz, I'm going to make whoever pay. I'm gonna make him wish that he had never cared about anyone as I snatch them all out of his life." And as much as Deuce didn't like the look in Killa's eyes or the message he had just delivered, he was gonna ride with his cousin regardless, because he had nothing but love and respect for Hulk as well.

The next few days seemed never ending, as friends and family made it their business to make sure Killa knew they were behind him 100 percent. Shit had gotten to the point where he wished it would be done and over with so that he could do what he needed to do, as his father had requested.

The morning came bright and full of life and sorrow as everyone prepared to get into the limos destined for the funeral home so they could pay their last respects to the person Killa now felt had been a great man. Before Killa's limo could pull off, a street team member ran up and banged on the window. Only two people in the car knew who this nigga was, and neither could understand why he was disrespecting their family's funeral.

After Spider got hold of his anger, he told Killa to let down the window. Killa, who was strapped, did so and pointed his gun in the nigga's face, as the dude said, "Yo, a limo just got swiss cheesed in front of the funeral home." The news was confusing to Killa, and it set off all kind of alarms in Spider's head.

Confused and worried, Spider repeated the dude's words to him: "So you're saying a couple of funny-sounding West Indians sprayed up a limo full of white people in front of Hulk's memorial?" Spider assumed that he knew who the white folks in that limo would've been, and that thought worried the shit out of him, but who did it—and why—scared the shit out of him even more. He thought, *Who would dare touch the Mob?*

And the mention of West Indian accents made it really confusing, because the Mob didn't fuck with West Indians at all. As much as they might hire outside their circuit, they would never have enrolled some West Indians to do that work.

Spider looked at Killa and said, "It's wartime, nephew. Are you ready?"

Furious about the disturbance of his family's grief, Killa answered by cocking his gun and yelling to the driver, "Plan B. Get us the fuck out of here." The memorial for his father would have to be delayed because of these latest developments. The police were all over that scene at the funeral home, and they wanted no part of the harassment.

All kinda phone calls were taking place. No one had all the answers, but the pieces were coming together, and the picture painted blood everywhere.

"Hello, Don. I know, I know," Vito's cousin Franky was saying into the phone, as a small army filled Vito's living room. "I told him about messing with those ungodly niggas. I'm on top of it, and all those involved will die. You can count on me, Don. Those niggas won't know what hit 'em."

As he hung up, Franky turned to the crowd and said in a low, menacing voice, "I want answers, and I want bodies. Doesn't have to be in that order, but I'd better have peace of mind by morning." Then he dropped to his knees and sobbed, in a room full of murderers.

While Killa was sitting on the window seat and looking like Malcolm X, Spider circled the floor, almost like he was digging a hole to get to the floor underneath them. Rage, confusion, and worry filled Spider with every lap he made around that tiny space. No one said a word, but they had a ton of questions and plans for revenge in their heads.

When the silence was broken, everyone could feel the heat from the question. "Who's Spraga, Unc?" Killa asked in a deliberately angry tone.

The question startled Spider and sent him into thoughts and memories he hadn't had in years. "Why?" he asked.

Killa rose and walked toward his uncle, looking like the grim reaper himself. "I know for a fact that he's been trying to kill my father for some time now. Why are you looking so surprised, Unc? Didn't think that I knew about him, huh? Well, your brother shared a lot of things with me, like you fucking his girl back in the day."

That statement shook Spider to his core and made him wonder what and how that situation had been explained to his nephew. Hulk and Spider had fought about that for a few years, and it was a bitter memory for Spider.

Staring into his uncle's eyes, Killa continued, "Yeah, Unc, I know everything, and I know that you're not built for this shit. My dad kept such a blanket around you that even though you were there, no one ever paid you any attention. You don't even have enough sense to have figured the shit out already. That's how much you've been in the fucking dark, living in your little brother's shadow."

Killa's words were daggers to Spider's heart, and the memories flooded his mind and suddenly made shit so clear. He couldn't bring himself to accept the fact that he'd never thought about that Jamaican who had started it all so long ago. Spider had become comfortable with life and the easy running of things. Now all he could do was collapse into a chair and hide his face in his hands as he continued to remember.

"If it's a war you want, make it start." These lyrics came blaring out of the speakers as Spraga skanked around. When Gully came in and saw how the boss man was acting, he would've thought it was his birthday.

Spraga caught Gully's eye and yelled over the music, "Good blood clot news, bredrin. Good bumba clot news, yes." Before Gully could process that, Spraga continued, "Ya see the pussy hole white boys dem ya kill, dat was dat pussy hole Vito." He kept skanking around the room while he spoke.

The name *Vito* sent Gully into his memories, and he realized that he had done a great thing by accident. He smiled and yelled, "Jah blessings and give thanks," as he began dancing with the boss man.

"How would ya feel if ya wake up one morning an saw a big M-16 nozzle at ya jaw," was blaring out of the speakers. Spraga said, "Yo, dem pussy holes couldn't a seen dat coming of blood clot sake. Me no see it, but Jah Rastafari run de world. You no see it? Yo, Gully, it's we time now fa truth." As he inhaled, he looked at Gully like a kid on Christmas and said, "Send fa Shareeda dem. Party time!"

Caught up in the victory of revenge, Spraga wasn't thinking about what he had done. He didn't care at the moment, but he soon would understand that it wasn't Jah's blessing, but a curse he should've let die a long time ago.

I guess Granny's fire for keeping me straight was dieting. When I got home, all I got was "Where were you?" A simple homecoming was the end of it. No ass whipping that night.

The next few months seemed to breeze by in a pretty regular way, with me headed to school, though not always making it there. Sometimes I went to my hood instead, and I reaped the benefits of being one of the crew. As much bullshit as my boys and I got into, the news and talk on the streets was mainly about a killing spree that had erupted in the Ville and East New York.

Not two hours passed before Franky's boys were bringing back information. "Hey, boss, we got word that it was some Jamaicans that shot up the limo." Franky's memory took him way back to when he used to fight with some Jamaicans out in Canarsie, until Vito had his boys handle the situation. *But damn, that was a lot of years ago*, he thought. *Naw, it can't be*. His mind started fucking with him, but then another one of his boys knocked at the door.

"Hey, boss, our guys over there said to talk to our guys at the Seventy-Third Precinct. They saw a car leaving their zone that could fit the description of who we're looking for. Our guys said that the only Jamaicans who could or would do something like that were called the Wet Them Up crew, led by a guy named Spraga. Does that make any sense to you?"

Franky's greatest fear had just become a reality. "Spraga, that fucking banana boat, funny- talking, monkey-looking …"

From their boss's reaction, the boys could tell they had retrieved the right information, which made their boss happy—even though it didn't show at the moment.

"Johnny, go get everything and everyone. We've got a reunion to bring together. I've got to say hello to an old friend," said Franky, with a sinister look on his face.

Killa knew what he had to do and who he had to do it to. "Check this out, Unc. My dad had already paid some dudes to come and deal with the situation when he saw the time being right. Ain't no time righter than now, but I'm going with them."

"Me too," said Deuce.

But Killa shook his head and said, "Unc, your ass *should* be the one going to take care of this shit, but I got this. Deuce says he's riding, too, so can't no shit go wrong." And with that, Killa laid out his plan for the hit.

Spraga, Gully, Juiceman, and Takedat were partying like it was New Year's Eve with Shreeda and her six friends. They had so much cocaine, marijuana, and alcohol in their systems that time didn't matter to them. They were on top of the world, and Spraga felt like he was Scarface himself. Never in his wildest dreams had he seen himself getting revenge on the two main contributions to the fire that had been lit in him so many years earlier.

But as that fire was lit, he had set a bomb that would blow up his entire existence. He had two sets of people looking to send him to hell—express. While Spraga was enjoying his victory, an all-out assault was being put together. He had no clue about what his future held, but he would soon find out.

At three o'clock on Monday morning, a car pulled up and parked on Ocean Avenue, and a second car parked on Dorchester right off Twenty-Second. A van stopped in front of an apartment building, and four men who looked like a SWAT team exited the vehicle. As they entered the lobby, they glimpsed a couple of men in the courtyard and took them out with two shots. Then they made their way up a few stairs to the first landing and stopped in front of an apartment door.

"I woulda let you go if you'd never dissed the program." Those words came through the door, bumping like there weren't any neighbors. The man on the other side of the door thought he heard something, but then he decided it must have been the loud music beating in his ears. He was on duty, so he was trying hard to resist the temptation to dance.

Kicking that lock felt like the easiest thing Killa had ever done. He slammed the door into the man standing behind it. Then the two hit men entered, put two in the guy's head, and watched him collapse on the floor. When the hit men saw what was going on in the room, they could've taken off their SWAT gear and just dropped their guns—if they hadn't been there in a professional capacity. Juiceman was bending over a big ass and killing it from behind. And if Takedat had opened his eyes, he could've seen his death coming—just as he was cumming, drilling a female in the plush chair underneath him. *Blam! Blam!* The sound of gunfire was the last thing they heard.

That sound must've hit Spraga and Gully simultaneously. They each jumped out of the pussies and opened their bedroom door. The sight of their faces with guns pointed directly at them would've been priceless. Behind the triggers of those two guns, Deuce and Killa wanted to do more than just kill the motherfuckers.

Before they could squeeze their triggers, Deuce and Killa heard two thumps. Someone had hit the floor behind them, and they turned to see two eyes staring at them through a ski mask. A brief standoff followed, with three guns pointing but nobody wanting to fire, except the two dudes caught with their pants down. As Killa and Deuce turned back to face their victims, two shots were fired from behind them—but they were still alive to talk about it. Spraga and Gully were dead, and the mystery killer had vanished.

Killa and Deuce hesitated slightly, but then realized that it was time to go. One headed toward Dorchester, and the other toward Ocean Avenue.

Two days had passed since his revenge was executed, but Killa didn't feel any better, and his life hadn't gotten any easier. In fact, he was preparing to let all of the skeletons out of the closet, after the funeral while everyone would be together. Brothers meeting each other for the first time, best friends finding out they were blood family, people looking the past in the face— everybody working together to bring about a brighter future.

Killa had a lot on his mind as he stood in front of the mirror, straightening his tie. The reality of his life's path had been set. He knew what he had to do and how he was going to do it. He recalled his father's words, "With great power comes great responsibility, son." Then the sound of a voice brought him out of his trance.

"Killa, someone's here to see you."

"Coming," Killa said. As he turned the corner and walked into his mother's living room, he saw those eyes again, the same eyes that he had seen two nights earlier for the first time.

Killa's hesitation made Franky smile. He reached out to shake Killa's hand as he introduced himself. "Hello, Killa. I'm Franky, a friend of your father's."

Killa shook Franky's hand and led him into the den, where they sat and talked. Throughout the conversation, not once was there any mention of what had taken place two nights earlier. But Killa learned a lot in that brief conversation, including the fact that he had a serious ally if he ever needed it.

"Again, my condolences to you and yours on the family lost. Anytime you need me, just call." With that, Franky rose, shook Killa's hand, and left with his two men.

When they were gone, Killa's mother entered. "Son, I know who you are. I know what you have, as well as what your father wanted you to do with it. I understand that you can't save everyone. But damn it, save yourself. I love you, and I don't want to bury you."

As she left the room, a tear came to Killa's eye. He wiped it away and made a promise to himself. *That's the last tear I'll shed behind this shit.*

Leo Moore

Life for me was pretty much everyday after that. I didn't see my man G-baby much anymore. I was still growing up and junior high had been wild, but I was headed to high school. It's funny how the forces of life all work together. What was yesterday becomes today in an instant.

www.ingramcontent.com/pod-product-compliance
Lightning Source LLC
Chambersburg PA
CBHW030201100526
44592CB00009B/385